SAINT MARTIN
DE PORRES

BOOKS BY MARY FABYAN WINDEATT

In This Series

Stories of the Saints for Young People ages 10 to 100

THE CHILDREN OF FATIMA
And Our Lady's Message to the World

THE CURÉ OF ARS
The Story of St. John Vianney,
Patron Saint of Parish Priests

THE LITTLE FLOWER
The Story of St. Therese of the Child Jesus

PATRON SAINT OF FIRST COMMUNICANTS
The Story of Blessed Imelda Lambertini

THE MIRACULOUS MEDAL
The Story of Our Lady's Appearances
to St. Catherine Labouré

ST. LOUIS DE MONTFORT
The Story of Our Lady's Slave,
St. Louis Mary Grignion De Montfort

SAINT THOMAS AQUINAS
The Story of "The Dumb Ox"

SAINT CATHERINE OF SIENA
The Story of the Girl Who Saw Saints in the Sky

SAINT HYACINTH OF POLAND
The Story of the Apostle of the North

SAINT MARTIN DE PORRES
The Story of the Little Doctor of Lima, Peru

SAINT ROSE OF LIMA
The Story of the First Canonized Saint of the Americas

PAULINE JARICOT
Foundress of the Living Rosary and
The Society for the Propagation of the Faith

SAINT MARTIN DE PORRES

THE STORY OF
THE LITTLE DOCTOR OF LIMA, PERU

By
Mary Fabyan Windeatt

Illustrated by
Sister Mary Jean Dorcy, O.P.

TAN BOOKS AND PUBLISHERS, INC.
Rockford, Illinois 61105

Nihil Obstat: Arthur J. Scanlan, S.T.D.
                 Censor Librorum

Imprimatur: ✠ Francis J. Spellman, D.D.
                 Archbishop of New York
                 New York
                 January 23, 1943

ISBN: 0-89555-423-2

Library of Congress Catalog Card No.: 93-83095

Printed and bound in the United States of America.

TAN BOOKS AND PUBLISHERS, INC.
P.O. Box 424
Rockford, Illinois 61105

1993

For
Reverend Norbert Georges, O.P.,
Director of the Blessed Martin Guild,
whose generous cooperation
made possible this little book.

CONTENTS

1. A Boy and a Beggar 1

2. Martin and Jane 10

3. The Little Doctor 19

4. Candles in the Dark 28

5. A New Job 37

6. Life at Santo Domingo 46

7. Vacation in the Country 56

8. The New Lay Brother 66

9. Martin and His Friends 74

10. A Busy Day 84

11. Martin's Young Neighbors 93

12. Martin Takes a Rest 102

13. Hero in Black and White 111

SAINT MARTIN DE PORRES

CHAPTER 1

A BOY AND A BEGGAR

THE ROYAL city of Lima, in the far-away country of Peru, lay shining like a jewel under a burning sun. The streets of the city were silent, for it was the hour of the noon-day siesta, when every house and shop closed its shutters against the burning heat.

But in the narrow street of Espiritu Santo, a young colored woman stood staring out of her open door. She had no time to rest. That was only for the wealthy folk, for grand *Señoras* who could ride about the city in golden carriages, and dress in the best of silk and lace.

"Oh, how I wish I could be a great lady!" she thought. "Then I wouldn't have to scrub and cook and wear old clothes. And my children could have a chance in life. But this way. . . ."

Poor Anna Velasquez! She was very unhappy in her small house, and even her little son and daughter brought her no pleasure. When she looked at Martin and Jane, playing together on the floor with their poor toys, she could have cried. What future

1

was there in the world for Negro children? In Lima the rich people said they were only fit to be servants.

"I'd rather be dead than live like this!" Anna often told herself. "If only I were white, and my babies white, then their father would never have left me. He would have been glad to stay here with us and build us a fine house."

The children's father, Don Juan de Porres, did not live with Anna. He was a very rich and powerful soldier, a Spanish gentleman with a fair complexion. He was also very proud and very handsome, and it pleased him that the King of Spain looked favorably upon him. The city of Lima belonged to Spain, as well as most of South America, and there were plenty of fine positions to be had for a man who remained in the King's favor. So now Don Juan looked at little Martin and Jane, and there was a shadow of disgust on his face. How could a knight in the King's service ever claim black-skinned children for his son and daughter? What a terrible blow it was that they resembled Anna instead of himself!

"I am going away on business," he told their mother presently. "I don't know when I shall be back. Here's some money for you and the children." And throwing a small bag of golden coins on the table, and with a fling of his grand scarlet cape, he was gone—whistling a lively tune as he went down the street to where his horse stood waiting.

Time passed. For many days Anna just stayed in her small house and cried. It seemed that Don Juan was ashamed of his own children! And what was Anna going to do when the money he had left her was used up?

Soon the little pile of golden coins had disappeared. There was nothing for Anna to do, if she did not wish to starve, but to get some work. And so, heartbroken and lonely, the young Negro mother finally decided to take in washing. It was the only kind of work she knew how to do. And as she scrubbed and scrubbed on the clothes, dreadful thoughts crept into her mind. She began to think it was a pity that Martin and Jane had ever been born.

"It's all their fault!" she thought. "If they had only been white children, like their father wished, he would never have left me to this awful life." And so, when little Martin or Jane came running to tell her that the Viceroy's golden carriage was coming down the street, or that there was going to be a great bonfire in the Plaza that night, Anna would only scowl.

"Go away, you little black brats! Can't you see I'm busy? Don't you know I haven't time for carriages or bonfires? It's all your fault we're so poor!"

It always made Martin sad to see his mother angry. Poor little boy, he could not understand what was so terrible about having black skin. There were all kinds of Negroes in Lima, and some of them very nice. And there were many nice Indians, too, whose skin was not a bit white. It was true, of course, that only the white or Spanish people in

Lima had money, but Martin did not believe that the noble Spanish ladies and gentlemen, whose carriages rolled so grandly past his mother's door, were really better than anyone else. Had he not heard the priest at the church say that God had made everyone in the world in His own image? That all men should be brothers? That Heaven was a place where Christians of all nations would be happy together?

"Mother has made a mistake," Martin told Jane one day. "It isn't the color of our skin that matters. It's the color of our souls. Jane, if we have white souls, if we do everything we can to please God, there's no need to feel sorry that we are only poor Negroes and that our father went away and left us."

Jane nodded. Martin was only a little older than she, but he was far more clever. He could speak so well, and everyone liked him. Even the dogs and cats that roamed the streets were his friends, and there was not one of them, even the wildest, that would not come when he called.

"I guess you're right, Martin. But it would be lovely to have a father who cared for us, and a nice house, and some nice clothes. Oh, Martin! I don't think I'd ever be unhappy again if I could have just one nice dress! A white silk dress, with some little red shoes to go with it!"

Martin and Jane grew quickly, even though many times they did not get enough to eat. They helped their mother around the house and it was always their job to take the clean laundry to the different houses. One warm day Anna called Martin to her. She had three small silver coins in one hand and a large empty basket in the other. She was very tired and hot, for she had been scrubbing since early morning. Now she looked closely at eight-year-old Martin.

"Can I trust you to go to the market and get something for dinner?" she asked. "You see, I know you, Martin. You'd give away every cent I make to beggars if I didn't watch you. But remember what happened the last time you tried that?"

Martin nodded gravely. A week ago his mother had been furious when he had put a silver coin into an old beggar's hat. On his return, without the loaves of bread she had sent him for, she had beaten him with a heavy stick. His body was still sore from the blows, but his mind had not forgotten the smile on the old beggar's face. It was the first time in a week, the old man had said, that anyone had given him an alms.

"I'll try not to give away any more money, Mother. Only it's hard to see poor old people hungry and not try to do something about it."

"Humph!" said Anna. "Let them work for a living, just as I do, if they want to eat. Now, take these three coins and do the best you can with them at the market. I want some bread, some beans and some fruit. Don't let anyone cheat you, and hurry home as fast as you can."

Martin smiled. He liked to be of use to his mother. "I'll run all the way," he said, and with the empty basket slung over one arm and the three silver coins clutched tightly in his hand, he ran out the door.

The sky was dull this morning, and the narrow street of Espiritu Santo crowded with people. Martin thought, as he ran, that the street was twice as full as it seemed, for every person in it, Negro or Indian or Spaniard, had a beautiful guardian angel at his side.

"How lovely it must look!" he thought, and if he had not been in such a hurry to reach the market, he would have gone into his favorite church of Santo Domingo and turned over this idea in his mind. But his mother was in a hurry for the food. He would put away the little thought he had just had and think about it some other time.

So on he ran, dodging peddlers with their wares, Indians with their donkeys, children with their dogs, until at last he reached the great Plaza de Armas. Upon this public square, that marked the center of the city, fronted the Cathedral and the palace of the Archbishop. Tall green palms grew here, and masses of colorful flowers. Here in the Plaza one could hear all the news and gossip of the day, for here rich men mingled with poor, discussing in loud voices all manner of topics.

The Plaza was an interesting place indeed, but Martin did not stop today. He had already passed on, his face flushed from running, when a pitiful voice sounded in his ear and a hand clutched his arm.

"An alms, child!" whined an old beggar woman, crouching on the rough stone sidewalk. "I have not eaten in three days...."

Martin's heart sank as he looked at the ragged creature. A beggar had found him, and he with three little coins in his hand!

"I am poor, my child. . .in God's Name. . .something for bread!"

Martin looked at the pitiful sight and shivered. Never had he seen such a tragic creature as this, a ragged shawl over her head, her eyes all but lost in the wrinkles of her face. He knew that his mother would all but kill him if he returned without the things she wished. But what could he do, when someone far poorer than himself was in need? He smiled a faint little smile and squared his shoulders.

"Here," he said, reaching for the old woman's bony hand, "take these three coins. And may God bless you!"

Then, so he would not hear the beggar woman's mumbled thanks, he turned and ran as swiftly as he could toward the church of Santo Domingo. Because he had not gone all the way to the market, he felt he could spare the time for a short visit. Before the tabernacle he would tell Our Lord that he had disobeyed his mother once more.

The church was cool and quiet. Two lay Brothers, in white habits with long black scapulars down the front and back, were sweeping one of the aisles. Martin went slowly toward the main altar and knelt down. He joined his hands and looked straight in front of him. He would tell his story just the way it had happened. And he would explain, too, how much he dreaded his mother's anger.

"TAKE THESE THREE COINS.
AND MAY GOD BLESS YOU!"

"She works so hard for her money, and I am always giving it away to beggars," he said softly. "Dear Lord, teach me always what is the right thing to do. And let me have a white soul, even if I am black on the outside. And bring my father back some day soon. And let me be brave when I tell Mother what I did with the three little coins. Amen."

CHAPTER 2

MARTIN AND JANE

MARTIN HAD been born in 1579 and Jane two years later. They had never gone to school. Since they were poor Negro children no one seemed to think it would be nice if they learned to read and write. In the great city of Lima, only the boys and girls of rich parents had a chance to learn anything. Martin did not mind too much that people thought him good-for-nothing, but it did make him feel sad to know that his father had gone away and his mother had to work so hard to support her little family.

"Where is Father?" Jane would often ask him. "Why doesn't he come back, Martin?"

Then the boy would try to explain that their father was a very important man, and traveled a great deal on business for the King of Spain.

"I wish he wasn't so busy," Jane would say. "I wish he didn't have to work, but could stay all the time with us. It would be so nice if he cared about us, Martin."

Martin agreed that it would be nice. "Maybe he

will come back some day," he said. "Let us pray for that."

Suddenly it happened. Don Juan de Porres returned to Lima, to Anna and her children. He had been many miles away, in the city of Guayaquil, Ecuador, to the north of Peru. While he was there, God had touched his heart and made him feel sorry about the way he had treated his little family.

"It's too bad that you've had such a hard time these past years," he told Anna. "I should have sent you more money for the children. Really, it's a shame that they have been going about in rags."

Anna was too happy to talk about the past. How good it was that Don Juan de Porres had not forgotten about them! And how grand he looked, in his fine clothes! The whole neighborhood was looking up to her, now that Don Juan had come back. She was no longer a poor working woman, but a really important person. Everyone knew that Don Juan had brought her a whole bag of gold, that he took Martin and Jane with him wherever he went, that he was terribly proud of both the children. But when they heard that he was going to take Martin and Jane with him to Ecuador and send them to school, there was even greater excitement.

"You mean we're really going to learn how to read, Father?" cried Jane. "Just like the rich white children? And we can have nice clothes to wear?"

"As many as you want. And money to spend, too. I want my boy and girl to do well in the world, and be a credit to me. You've been beggars long enough."

Jane could not believe her ears. Anna was beside herself with joy. And Martin? Martin could not thank God enough for the wonderful days of happiness that had suddenly become his lot.

Don Juan stayed in Lima for several weeks, but before long he received word to travel to the north. His uncle, Don Diego de Miranda, was anxious he should come to Guayaquil at once. There was a lot of work there needing his attention. So Martin and Jane, very fine in brand-new clothes, said good-bye to their mother. Friends and neighbors for blocks around came to wish them well. Anna did not know whether to laugh or to cry. For so many years she had had to work and slave to keep her little home together. Many times she had almost hated her children, because their black skin had been the reason for Don Juan leaving her. But now, well, she was sorry to see them go. In spite of all the times she had punished Martin for giving away her money to the poor, she really loved the little boy. And she loved Jane, too.

"Be sure you aren't a trouble to your father," she warned them. "He's a great man in the King's service, and you want to act so that he won't be ashamed of you."

"We'll be good, Mother," said Martin. "Don't worry."

"We'll remember everything you've told us," put in Jane. "Isn't it wonderful that we have the chance to go to school?"

Anna nodded. It was wonderful. In the whole street of Espiritu Santo, where the children had been born, not one person had ever learned to read or write. Such things were only for the wealthy, not for poor Negroes. But now here were Martin and Jane, so happy and splendid in their new clothes that she hardly knew them. And they were on their way to Ecuador, to their father's rich uncle in Guayaquil! Truly, it was like a dream, thought Anna. And then, because she suddenly knew she was going to cry, she kissed Martin and Jane in a great hurry and ran into the house. Don Juan was still inside. She wanted to have a few words with him away from all the curious eyes of the neighbors.

When Martin and Jane had left Lima and gone the few miles to the harbor of Callao, where a boat was waiting to take them to the north, they felt a little strange. Never had either of them been so far away from home before. Never had they dreamed there could be so many different people, or so many wonderful ships as those which lay at anchor in the harbor. Great sails flapped idly in the wind on the big wooden vessels. Black men, yellow men and white men crowded about, talking excitedly in strange tongues. There was much going and coming. Martin was particularly interested in the scores of Negro slaves whose backs were bent under great bundles, who journeyed from shore to ship and from ship to shore without ever stopping to rest.

"Father, what are the black men carrying in those big bundles?" he asked. "And where are all these ships going?"

Don Juan laughed. "They are carrying gold, son. And the ships are going to Spain, on the King's service."

"Oh," said Martin, and did not ask any more questions.

How well he knew about the gold and silver that came down from the mountains beyond the city of Lima! The Spaniards, who had invaded Peru some forty-five years before he had been born, were very fond of gold and silver. They were so fond of it that they made thousands of poor Indians and Negroes go to work for them in the mines. This would not have been as bad if the Spaniards had only been kind masters. But many of them were cruel, and did not think of the poor people who had to work for them. Right now many Indians and Negroes were dying of hardship in the mines, so that ships like these in the harbor of Callao could take riches to Spain.

"It is not right," thought the little boy. "People should not be unkind to one another, or be greedy for gold. I am sure that God must feel sad that these poor Negroes have to work so hard." And there were tears in his eyes as he looked at the Spanish ships, into whose great holds the precious cargo of gold was being loaded.

But there was not much time to stand watching the ships. Don Juan suddenly realized that he and the children would be late for their own boat if they did not hurry.

"Come along," he said. "Take Jane's hand, Martin, and follow me. Our boat is over this way."

Martin and Jane enjoyed the long voyage to Guayaquil. When they reached the city, they found Don Diego de Miranda, their father's uncle, waiting to greet them. Don Diego was an old man, with white hair, but he had a kind face. Jane liked him right away, and so did Martin. But Don Diego stared at the two children in a rather curious manner.

"Why, who are you?" he asked. "Don't tell me you're lost!"

Don Juan de Porres laughed as though he thought this a great joke. "*Lost?* Why, these are *my* children, Uncle! The boy's name is Martin and the girl is called Jane. Their mother is in Lima just now, as I wrote you. I brought the children along with me, hoping you could arrange for them to have a little schooling."

Don Diego stared at the two black-skinned children before him, then at Don Juan. There was a strange look on his face, and Martin's heart started to beat faster. He knew what Don Diego was thinking:

All my other relatives are white, but these children are black!

Martin felt the old sadness stealing over him again. Why, oh why, did a person's color matter so much? Surely God loved the soul of his black mother as much as He did that of his white father. Don Juan, however, was not in the least disturbed by the strange look on Don Diego's face.

"They are good children," he said. "I know they will do what they are told and not be a bother to you. All I ask is that you give them a good home and see that they get an education—for my sake!"

Martin, holding very tight to Jane's hand, ventured a smile at the old man in the fine clothes. "We'll work very hard," he said. "We won't be any trouble."

Strangely enough, at the boy's words Don Diego's face suddenly broke into a smile. "As my own great-nephew and niece, you are most welcome to Guayaquil," he said. "You say you want to go to school?"

Jane was no longer afraid of Don Diego. "Oh, please, we should love that! We've talked about nothing else ever since we left home!"

"That's true enough," said Don Juan. "And I am particularly anxious to give the boy a chance to get ahead. He's quite a good worker, Uncle. I think he deserves a chance."

Don Diego bowed. "I shall see that they have a private tutor," he said. "The best will be none too good for my own flesh and blood. But why are we standing here talking? The three of you must be tired. My carriage is waiting and we can talk just as well at home. Come along, children."

Martin and Jane were very happy in Guayaquil. It was indeed a new thing for them to have a nice home, plenty to eat, good clothes to wear and a teacher who came every day to give them lessons. They worked very hard, and it was not long before each of them knew all the letters of the alphabet. Martin was a little quicker than Jane at his lessons, for he was eight years old and she only six, but they both did their best and their father and great-

A TEACHER CAME EVERY DAY
TO GIVE THEM LESSONS.

uncle were very pleased.

"Didn't I tell you that they were good children?" said Don Juan one day. "Didn't I tell you they would be no trouble to you?"

Don Diego nodded his white head. "You did," he said. "But what you didn't say was that these children would change my whole life. The house hasn't been the same since Martin and Jane came. It's such a happy place now, with those two young ones around to cheer me up!"

CHAPTER 3

THE LITTLE DOCTOR

MARTIN STAYED in Guayaquil for two years, a very happy boy indeed. Jane and he could read and write well, and their sad life in Lima seemed like a dream. Don Diego was very kind to both children, and they also saw a lot of their father, the dashing Don Juan de Porres. The days were very different from the old ones at home, when frequently Martin and Jane had not even had enough to eat.

"Oh, I like it here in Uncle's house so much!" Jane said one day. "But Martin, we do have to go home some time, don't we? We can't stay here forever?"

"No, I suppose not," replied Martin. "And we have to think about Mother, Jane. She must be rather lonely away down in Lima by herself."

Jane nodded. "Two years is a long time to be gone. But still, perhaps we can stay just a little while longer, Martin. I think Uncle likes us a lot. He never says anything about our going away."

It was true. Don Diego de Miranda had become

very fond of his nephew's children. He would have
kept them with him willingly. But one day there
was great excitement in the house. Don Juan de
Porres had been named Governor of Panama! In a
very short time he would have to leave Guayaquil
for his new and important position in the north. But
before he went, he would have to make a short visit
to Lima.

Don Juan was very pleased about his new position, but when he looked at the children some of
the joy faded. He could not take his son and daughter with him this time, for he would be very busy
in Panama and he had no relatives there who would
look after Martin and Jane. Besides, perhaps it was
best for Martin to go home to his mother. He was
getting to be a big boy now, and would be a comfort
to Anna. As for Jane, Don Juan had other plans.
Although she was only eight years old, she gave
promise of turning into a capable woman. In a few
more years she would make some man a good wife.

As well as he could, Don Juan broke the news
to his little son and daughter. Jane was to stay in
Guayaquil with Don Diego, who would find her a
good husband when the time came. Martin was to
return to his mother in Lima. Perhaps a little later
he could also start to learn a trade.

"What would you like to be, lad?" his father
asked. Martin did not have to think very hard, for
he had always had a dream in his heart.

"I should like to be a doctor, Father," he replied.
"I should like to know how to make sick people
well."

Don Juan laughed at the serious look on the ten-year-old boy's face, but he was pleased just the same.

"That's fine," he said. "You shall learn to be a doctor, Martin. Back in Lima I know the very man who will teach you. His name is Dr. Marcelo de Rivero."

When Martin returned to his native city, he found that his mother was no longer living in the little house in the street of Espiritu Santo. Instead, she was making her home with Doña Francisca Velez Miquel, close to the church of San Lazaro. She and Doña Francisca were good friends, and they welcomed Martin with open arms.

"My, how you have grown!" cried Anna, the first time she saw Martin. "Why, you are almost as tall as I am!"

"I can hardly believe my eyes!" exclaimed Doña Francisca. "Anna, you must be so proud to have such a fine-looking son!"

Martin smiled at his mother, sensing that she had changed since he had gone away. There was something different now in the way she looked at him. It was almost as if she were a little bit afraid of him, now that he had seen some of the world, now that he had had some education and knew how to read and to write. Could it be that she would not punish him again if he gave away money to the poor? Could it be that she was really proud of him at last, now that she knew Marcelo de Rivero was to teach him to be a doctor?

"It's good to be home," he said. "Mother, I'm so

glad I'll soon be able to earn a little money for you. I want so much to be useful—if I can!"

There were tears in Anna's eyes as she looked at the boy before her, so straight and tall and strong. "God bless you," she murmured, holding him close to her. "God help you in your new work."

The months passed, and Martin left the house of Doña Francisca, where his mother still lived. He had become Dr. de Rivero's assistant, and every day was learning more and more about how to cure the sick. He lived in a house close to his work, a house belonging to a lady called Ventura de Luna. Each morning he got up very early and went to hear Mass at the church of San Lazaro. Although he was just a Negro boy, and the rich white people in the town paid him little attention, he knew that God loved him. God had thought so much of him, and of every other poor Negro in the world, that He had given each a soul that could never die. Now black people had extra sufferings to bear, but there would come a day when all the cruelty and injustice would be at an end. In Heaven there would be no one to care about the color of one's skin, or about the other things that mattered so much on earth. All that would matter in Heaven would be how well one had done his duty on earth, how faithfully one had loved God and done His Will.

God's Will! Martin often used to think about that, as he knelt in the church of San Lazaro every morning, and watched the priest offer Holy Mass. What was God's Will for those who lived on earth? Wasn't it to love one another, because in every human body there is a soul that is the image of God Himself?

"If I love people, and try to make them happy, I am really loving God and making Him happy," Martin decided. "How glad I am that I was born! How glad everybody should be that they are living in this world, with a chance to do God's Will and then go to live with Him forever in Heaven! And what a pity so few people see it this way!"

Martin loved his new life. Before six months had passed, his employer, Dr. de Rivero, was telling his friends that he had never known such a trustworthy boy.

"His hands seem to know just what to do for the sick," he said. "And his memory? Well, it's simply remarkable! That lad can make up any medicine, no matter how difficult. Why, he's even learned how to set a broken bone!"

It was true. Martin liked nothing better than to work around the little shop of his employer. Here were many shelves, each reaching to the ceiling, and each holding rows and rows of bottles. The bottles were all shapes and sizes, holding brightly colored liquids and powders. These were the medicines which the doctor made out of herbs and plants. In only a short time, Martin knew all these medicines by name. He liked to look at the different bottles and to realize that they held comfort and relief for those who were sick.

One morning the boy was alone in the shop, for Dr. de Rivero had gone to the other side of the city to visit a sick man. As usual, Martin was busy. He

"DON'T WORRY," HE WHISPERED.
"YOU'RE GOING TO BE ALL RIGHT."

swept the shop, dusted the tables, the chairs, the shelves with their bottles, and was hanging up a large bunch of herbs to dry when he heard a terrible commotion in the street. Two Indians had been fighting farther up the block, and one of them was bleeding badly from a great cut over the eyes. Martin looked out of the door and saw that the wounded man was being carried toward the shop.

"Quick! Where is Dr. de Rivero?" cried a woman who had run ahead of the others. "This poor Indian is bleeding to death!"

"The doctor isn't here," said Martin. "But don't worry. I'll look after the man."

The woman tossed a scornful look at the boy. "This is no time for jokes," she said. "Quick! Tell me where there is another doctor's shop!"

Martin was very calm. "There wouldn't be time to go for anyone else," he said. "Here, help me open the door so they can bring the poor man inside."

"But you're only a child!" cried the woman. "Don't you see that this is a matter of life and death?"

"Yes," said Martin. "I see."

The Indian was brought in and laid upon a couch, and everyone was amazed to see how Martin at once took command of the situation. In an instant he had some water in a basin, a sponge in his hand and some strange, sweet-smelling white powder in a little dish. He bent over the man, who was moaning with pain, and went quietly to work.

"Don't worry," he whispered. "You're going to be all right."

The people who had crowded into the shop were silent as they watched the twelve-year-old Martin go about his work. Where had a mere boy learned such gentle skill? Scarcely had he washed the dreadful wound with water and put the white powder on it than the bleeding began to stop.

"Who is this little Negro?" whispered the woman who had first run into the room. There was wonder now, not scorn, in her voice.

"He is Martin de Porres," someone replied, "Dr. de Rivero's apprentice. And a good one, too, by the look of things."

In a few minutes Martin had finished his work. The deep cut was now covered with a clean white cloth, and the man was able to sit up and look around.

"There," said the boy. "You're all right now. Just remember to be quiet and rest. And if you'll come in tomorrow, I'll put on a clean bandage. In the meantime, you might take this along with you."

The Indian took the little bottle of liquid that Martin handed to him and looked at it curiously. It was deep red in color.

"What's this?" he asked.

"Wine," answered Martin. "You've had a bad shock, and a little drink of wine will help you to feel better."

One by one the people left the doctor's house and went out into the street. Two of them took the wounded man by the arm to lead him home. But the others remained, talking in little groups about the remarkable scene they had just witnessed.

"That lad's a marvel!" said one man. "I don't think the doctor himself could have done a better job. For myself, I'm afraid that the sight of all that blood would have made me lose my nerve."

"Young Martin de Porres doesn't know what fear is," put in another. "Why, I've seen him fix up many cases that were far worse than this. . . ."

CHAPTER 4

CANDLES IN THE DARK

VENTURA DE LUNA was fond of Martin. He caused her no trouble at all, and she often wished she could rent her other rooms to equally good tenants.

"But where can I find another Martin de Porres?" she sighed. "There is not another like him anywhere."

Martin, in turn, was happy in his new home. He did not spend much time there, since his work for Dr. de Rivero kept him busy from morning until late at night. Still, he liked his little room, and when the day's work was done it was good to have a place to go to that was all his own. However, there was a flaw. Ventura never left him any candles, which meant that when he came home late at night, his room was always dark. He could hardly see his bed, or the small table where he kept his few books.

"I'd like to buy some of your candles," he told Ventura one day. "Could I please have a few of the ones that are nearly used up?"

Ventura was surprised. Martin had never asked her for anything before. From the day he had first come to live with her, he had never made one complaint about his room, the food, or the way she washed his clothes.

"Of course you can have some candles," she told him quickly. "There's a box full of them out in the kitchen. But you don't have to buy those old stumps of wax, Martin. You can have all you want for nothing."

The boy was delighted, and that night, when he came home from the shop, he lit one of the small candles and looked about the little room that had been his home ever since the day he had become Dr. de Rivero's apprentice. It was a plain little place, with one small window that faced the garden. From this window he could see the little lemon tree he had planted for Ventura some days before. It was just a slip of a plant now, but every night he prayed that it would grow into a good tree some day, and give glory to God because it was useful and full of beauty.

But Martin spent little time that night thinking about the lemon tree in Ventura's garden. The flickering flame of the small candle lit up his room and he looked about him curiously. It looked so different by candlelight. There was his bed, in the corner by the window; there were his chair, his table, the few books he owned, the sturdy wooden chest which Don Diego de Miranda had once given him, and in which he kept his clothes. Everything was very plain and simple. The floor was of rough brick,

the walls of white plaster, not at all like the room
he had had when he was living in Guayaquil with
his great-uncle.

"I like this place," the boy thought. "I like it very
much."

He sat down in his chair and stared at the oppo-
site wall. Ventura had put a small wooden crucifix
there, above the head of his bed, and the moving
light of the candle cast strange shadows over the
figure of Our Lord. It was almost as though He
were alive. And as he sat there, looking at the crucifix, strange thoughts came into the boy's mind.
Outside a little wind sprang up, rustling the ragged
palm trees that grew in Ventura's garden. But Martin did not notice the wind. He did not hear the
laughter of passers-by in the street, or the rumbling
of an occasional carriage on its way home from a
ball at the Viceroy's palace. He was thinking of Our
Lord and how He had suffered so much on earth.
First He had been born in a stable. Then He had
grown up in a poor little house in Nazareth. When
He was older, even His best friends had been afraid
to stay with Him. Then He had died on a cross.

"Why was it like this?" asked Martin, looking at
the crucifix. "Why did You do so much?"

Presently the boy slipped on his knees and hid
his face in his hands. He knew why Our Lord had
been poor and lonely and with so few real friends.
He knew why He had died. It was to give Heaven
to mankind, to people of every nation. It was to
make God's holiness and love win a victory over sin
and the devil.

As Martin knelt beside his bed, in the glow of the dying candle, his heart filled with thanks. How wonderful it was to think about God's love, the way He had made billions and billions of souls in His own likeness, how He had made places for everyone near Himself in Heaven, how He had made it possible for all men to go there, even after Adam and Eve had thrown away the chance!

"Thank You for my place in Paradise," whispered Martin. "Thank You for everything You did."

The months passed, and Martin was as busy as ever at the shop. He loved his work and was pleased when he saw that he was learning to be useful. But the thought never left him of the greatness of God's love, and how He had given Himself to ransom mankind.

"I should like to give myself for a great work, too," the boy thought. "I should like to spend my whole life in making people understand what God has done for them. But oh, Lord! You tell me how this is to be! You tell me how I can keep very close to You, and use myself in Your service!"

It was not so very long before Ventura de Luna became puzzled about Martin. There was always a light burning in his room at night, and the candles she so often gave him were used in no time.

"That boy should not be reading so much," she told herself. "After working all day at the shop, he should get his proper rest."

But was Martin reading every night in his little room? Was this really the reason that he used so many candles? Ventura was not sure, but she determined to find out. Early one morning she crept up silently to Martin's door. A faint ray of light was streaming through a crack, although the rest of the household had been long deep in slumber. Silently she stood outside the door, then peered through the keyhole. What she saw made her heart beat fast. Her young friend was not reading. He was kneeling beside his bed, in front of the crucifix, and there were tears streaming down his face.

"Mother of God!" thought the good woman. "So this is what he is doing! *Praying!*"

In the three years that followed, Martin did not know that Ventura often watched him at prayer. Indeed, as he grew older, he was interested in only one thing and that was what he should do with his life.

By the time he was fifteen years old, he had decided to stop being Dr. de Rivero's helper. Instead, he would offer his services to the priests at the Dominican convent in Lima. This, he felt sure, was what Our Lord wished. This was the work for which he had been born. However, he would not be a priest, or even a lay Brother. He would be just a helper in the monastery, doing odd jobs about the place that were too small for anyone else.

"You gave Yourself to me, I will give myself to You," Martin said. "Lord, just let me help people who are tired and sick and unhappy. Just let me make them see how much You love them!"

Martin's decision to go and live at the convent of Santo Domingo was a great surprise to everyone.

Dr. de Rivero was terribly upset.

"For three years you've been with me, Martin, the very best boy I ever had. What am I going to do now all by myself? What am I going to say to the patients?"

Martin smiled. He would miss the little shop, with its crowded hall where the sick people waited for the doctor, the little back room where he had learned how to mix the native herbs and grind them into healing medicines. But God was calling him now to a different life. Nothing else mattered.

"I'm sure you'll find another boy to help you," he told the doctor. "And thank you so much for everything you've done for me. Without you, what should I have ever known about medicine?"

The next few days Martin was very busy saying good-bye to his friends. Of course he was not going very far away. He would still be living in the city of Lima, but once he was a servant at the Dominican convent his time would no longer be his own. He would not be able to go and come as he pleased. His mother, the doctor, Ventura de Luna, Doña Francisca and the priests of the church at San Lazaro (where he had been hearing Mass each morning for the past three years) promised to come and see him often.

"Oh, how I'm going to miss you!" Anna said. "It's hard on a mother to lose her only son, Martin. And I don't see why you only want to be a servant for the Dominicans. Why couldn't you ask to be a lay Brother, or even a priest?"

Martin had expected his mother to feel like this,

HE WOULD OFFER HIS SERVICES
TO THE DOMINICAN PRIESTS.

and his father, too, when the news of his entrance into the monastery finally reached him at Panama. He knew his parents were proud of him, and of his success at the doctor's shop these last three years. He was no longer an ignorant little boy. He could read and write, and his skill in caring for the sick was well known to many in Lima. Now that he was fifteen years old, and just ready for an interesting career, why did he only want to be the least among those who lived at Santo Domingo?

"Dear Mother, I don't care about being important," Martin said. "I don't think God would ever choose me for the big things in life. He has other souls instead. But He needs people to do little things for Him, too, and so I have offered myself as a servant at the monastery. Won't you pray for me, that I may serve Him well there?"

Anna did not know what to say. She was both happy and sad at Martin's choice. Suddenly she wondered if Martin had already gone to see Father Francis Vega, the Prior at Santo Domingo. Had her son really been accepted by the Dominican priests? Or was he only thinking about going away?

Martin seemed to sense what was going on in his mother's mind. "Last week I went to see Father Francis Vega," he said. "I told him how I wanted to live with the Fathers and work about the convent. He said he would let me know about it later. Today, Mother, there was a message from him. I am to go next week!"

Martin's face was bright with happiness. Looking at him, Anna had to admit that her own heart was slowly filling with a strange joy. What was there about this lad of hers that set him apart from other youngsters in the neighborhood? Was it true, as Ventura de Luna had once told her, that Martin was really very holy?

CHAPTER 5

A NEW JOB

WHEN MARTIN went to live at the convent of Santo Domingo, he put aside his ordinary clothes and started to wear a religious habit. It was made of white wool, something on the style of that worn by the priests and lay Brothers, although without the long scapular down the front and back. Around his neck he wore a large rosary. Some of those at Santo Domingo were surprised to see that Martin also had another rosary hanging from his leather belt, but the Father Prior did not mind. He was quite pleased with the Negro boy who was said to have such a wonderful skill with the sick. There was no doubt he would be useful in his new home.

"You'll probably find things a little strange here at first," the Prior said kindly. "Perhaps it would be best if we gave you just small duties in the beginning. Now, how are you at cutting hair, Martin? Do you think you could be a barber?"

Martin nodded eagerly. "Oh, yes, Father! I've often cut people's hair. When I was with Dr. de

Rivero. . . ."

The Prior smiled. "That's right. I had forgotten the good man is a barber as well as a surgeon. Well, Martin, you will have charge of all the hair cutting here. Since there are over two hundred of us, it will keep you fairly busy. Later we shall see what other things you can do. Now run along to Brother Vincent. He will give you some shears and show you just how to cut the priests' and Brothers' hair."

So Martin hurried off through the corridor in search of Brother Vincent. His heart was very light. Oh, how good it was to be here in a monastery, where everyone was pledged to God's service! He must never forget to thank God for the gift of his vocation.

For the first week Martin did quite well as the convent barber. Brother Vincent had told him just how he should cut the priests' and Brothers' hair, and he managed to please all those who came to him. But one morning he found that Brother James was waiting for a haircut. Brother James was a very particular young man, a student for the priesthood. He came from a wealthy family in Lima, and everyone at Santo Domingo knew that he was clever at books and someday would make a name for himself as a great scholar.

"I haven't very much time, Martin," Brother James said as he came into the room where Martin was waiting. "Give me a haircut as fast as you can, please."

Martin nodded, and took out his shears. Brother James sat down by the window and began to read the book which he had brought with him. He paid no attention to Martin's efforts, and seemed interested only in the volume he was reading. From time to time he smiled to himself, and made little notes in the margins. But when a distant bell suddenly started to ring, he shut his book with a bang.

"Aren't you through yet?" he asked sharply.

"That's the bell to get ready for prayers."

Martin shifted from one foot to another. "I'll just be another minute, Brother. There's a tiny bit here in front...."

But Brother James was suddenly standing erect, feeling his newly clipped head, and his face was a deep crimson. His book fell unheeded to the floor. "Why, you little fool!" he cried. "You've hardly left me any hair at all! Oh, I should have had more sense than to let you try your hand on me! Don't you know I like my hair long on the sides and short at the back?"

Martin lowered his eyes. "I'm sorry, Brother James."

"_Sorry?_ I should think you would be sorry! Whoever made a child like you the community barber? Little Negroes would be better off in the barn, looking after the cattle!"

Martin flushed. "I know I'm not much good," he said. "But I tried to cut your hair the way the rule says, Brother James. You know everyone here is supposed to have his hair cut the same way—short all around."

Brother James sniffed. "Don't argue with me," he said. "I always have my hair cut the way I like it.

And no little Negro is going to tell _me_ what the rule says!"

Martin was troubled. He knew he was in the right, but he had no desire to make people angry and offend God. Perhaps an apology. . .

"Brother James, I'm terribly sorry I've displeased you," he said. And before the other could stop him, he was down on his knees to kiss his feet. Then, with a little smile, he got up.

"I have a nice orange here," he said. "Will you put it in your pocket and eat it when you have a little free time?"

In the distance the bell began to ring again. Brother James looked scornfully at the boy before him. "Humph!" he said, and went quickly out of the room.

The door slammed behind him, and Martin sighed. Brother James was still angry. As he started to sweep up the hair which had fallen to the floor, he wondered what Brother James would say the next time he came for a haircut.

"Because I shall cut it just the same way," he told himself. "Now that I am living at Santo Domingo, I must not be afraid of what people think of me, or the cross things they say. Nothing matters, except keeping the rule of the convent."

Martin had trouble with a few other Brothers, who had their own ideas about haircuts, but he kept on doing as the Prior wished. Gradually every priest and Brother in the convent came to realize that it was no use to argue with the black-skinned youth who was the community barber. It was

MARTIN CAME TO HAVE MANY DUTIES.

common knowledge that he would rather die than break a rule, and so finally even Brother James became resigned to having his hair cut short all around.

Besides being the barber at Santo Domingo, Martin came to have other duties. He was just fifteen years old when he first came to the monastery to be a servant, and he never asked to have things easy. As the years passed, the Prior told Martin he would do other things besides cut hair. He would have charge of the clothesroom in the monastery and he would also be in charge of the sick.

"Thank you, Father Prior," said Martin. "I just hope I'm able to look after all these duties well."

"You'll do all right," said the Prior. "By the way, I might as well tell you about Father Peter Montesdosca. He's in a bad way, Martin. You'll want to give him very special care, now that you're in charge of the sick people here."

"I know he has a badly infected leg, Father."

"It's worse than you think, Martin. He's going to lose that leg, because that's the only way to save his life. And what a fuss he's making about it, poor soul! Perhaps you'd better go and see him now. Maybe you can make him feel more cheerful."

As Martin started off toward Father Peter's room, a sudden idea struck him. Maybe Father Peter would like something nice to eat. That was often the case with invalids. And if he could get something very special from the kitchen, perhaps the poor sick priest would be in a better humor.

"Dear Lord, please give me an idea of what

Father Peter would like," said Martin. "Put into my mind the thing that will please him most."

It was strange, but as Martin breathed his little prayer the thought came to him that perhaps Father Peter would like a salad...some green vegetables, with a little seasoning, and perhaps a few capers, those buds from the prickly green shrubs that grew in the convent garden, which had such a nice flavor. Yes, that's what he would bring Father Peter. A salad with capers.

"Thank You, dear Lord, for the idea," whispered Martin, and started off to the kitchen to prepare the salad for the invalid.

In just a few minutes the tasty dish was ready, and Martin was opening the door of Father Peter's room. It was dark in here, but he could make out a figure in bed. In fact, he did not need his eyes to tell him there was someone in the room, for Father Peter was groaning loudly.

"Oooh! My leg! My leg! Go away, whoever you are! Let me die!"

Martin smiled to himself, then tip-toed over to the bed. "Father, it's just Martin," he said softly.

"*Martin?* I don't care who it is. I want to be left alone!"

"Shall I open the shutters, Father? You'd feel so much better if there were a little sunlight in here."

"I tell you, leave me alone! I don't want to see anything or anyone! Not when I'm in such misery!"

"But Father! I brought you something."

"Well, take it away, boy! Ooooh...my leg! My leg!"

"Dear Father, I brought you a nice fresh salad, with capers. Won't you even look at it?"

At these words the figure in the bed turned over, very slowly. "A salad? Did you say you brought me a *salad?*"

"Yes, Father Peter. I made it myself just a few minutes ago. Could you...that is...wouldn't you...like to try it?"

Father Peter leaned back against his pillows with a little sigh. "Open the shutters," he ordered. "Then let me see this salad. How did you guess that's what I've been wanting all day, boy?"

Martin opened the shutters, so that the sunlight filled every corner of the sickroom, then placed the bowl of salad in Father Peter's eager hands. "Why, I just hoped for the best," he said. "I offered a little prayer, Father, that I would please you. That's all."

The sick priest took a doubtful taste of the salad, then another. Martin watched him anxiously. "Is it good, Father? Do you really like it?"

A smile crossed Father Peter's pain-lined face. "It's the best salad I ever ate," he said. "You must make me another tomorrow."

Martin offered a quick prayer of thanks for having been able to please this sick priest. But then his eyes lighted upon the latter's sore leg. It was wrapped in yards and yards of linen, and the Prior had said it was so badly diseased that very soon it would have to be cut off. What a terrible thing for poor Father Peter! How could he ever go about his priestly duties with only one leg? How could he ever say Holy Mass?

"Maybe something can be done," the boy thought. "God is always so wonderful, when people have faith in Him...."

CHAPTER 6

LIFE AT SANTO DOMINGO

A FEW HOURS after Martin had brought him the salad, Father Peter was beside himself with joy. The painful swelling was beginning to leave his leg. When the boy came to see him later that night, the priest was no longer in bed but walking about the room.

"Martin, I'm cured! This afternoon, just after you left, something wonderful happened. My leg became all right. Oh, my son! You did it! You made me well! How am I ever going to thank you?"

Martin's dark eyes shone. It was true. Father Peter's sore leg was sore no longer. There would be no need to cut it off now. Oh, how wonderful that God had heard the prayers he had been offering for Father Peter! Yet it was wrong that the priest should be thanking him this way, should be thinking he had done anything of himself.

"Father, don't praise me for your cure," he said quickly. "I didn't do anything but make you a salad and wash your leg with a little plain water. You know that."

"Plain water? I think there was more than that to it, Martin."

"Plain water and a clean bandage," said Martin laughing. "Anyone could have done the same for you, Father."

"Then how is it that I am cured, when for months this leg has been so sore? Answer me that."

Martin smiled, and began to straighten out Father Peter's bed. "God must love you a lot," he said. "Only He could have cured you so quickly, Father. Now, is there anything you would like me to bring you before I go to bed? Some fruit, perhaps? Or something to drink?"

Father Peter laughed. "I can wait on myself now," he said. "Dear Martin, I'm well again! I'm able to walk about as well as I ever did. Forgive me for the cross words I've said to you. When I think how many times I have scolded you, called you a useless boy. . ."

"You were only speaking the truth," replied Martin with a smile. "But I'm glad you are well again, Father. So very glad!" And before Father Peter could say another word, Martin had slipped out the door.

At five o'clock the next morning, young Martin was awakened by the heavy pealing of the bell in the monastery tower. Another day was about to begin, another collection of hours in which to love God and serve those about him. Quickly Martin arose from his hard bed. As was the custom in the convent, he had slept fully dressed, except for his shoes. He found these now and put them on, then paused a moment to look at the crucifix on his wall. It was still very dark, but outside the chilly air was already echoing to the sounds of many other church bells in the city. There, just a few blocks away, were the deep-throated bells of the Cathedral. On a higher pitch, and slightly more distant, were those of the Franciscan convent. As Martin listened, the whole world seemed full of the sound of bells. In the tower of the convent of La Merced, the music of sounding bronze was calling the white-clad sons of St. Peter Nolasco to prayer. Over to the right, the bells of San Sebastian (the church where he had been baptized) were adding their voices to the holy music that rang out over the royal city of Lima each morning.

"Praised be Jesus Christ!" said Martin, looking at the crucifix. Then he glanced briefly at the pictures of the Blessed Virgin and St. Dominic which hung upon his wall. It was too dark to see them clearly, but the boy had no need of that. Each morning he paused briefly to look at his two heavenly friends and to ask their help during the day. He had been doing that ever since he had come to Santo Domingo, and this morning was no exception.

"Dear Blessed Mother, let me be useful this day," he whispered. *"Holy Father St. Dominic, help me in my work. St. Joseph, pray for all of us in this monastery, and keep us from harm."*

He opened his door and started quietly down the hall. Each morning he served Mass for one of the Dominican priests. Sometimes it was in the convent itself, in one of the several chapels. Today it was to be at the Rosary altar in the public church that was attached to the monastery. Martin remembered, as he went quickly along the chilly corridor, how he had often prayed at this altar of Our Blessed Lady when he had been a little boy. How many times he had come here when he knew his own mother was angry with him for having given money to the poor! But he had never dreamed that someday he would be serving Mass at this very altar, dressed in the black and white habit of the Dominican Order. How strange were God's ways, and how wonderful!

The Holy Sacrifice proceeded, with Martin answering the prayers of the priest in the Latin he had learned so well. As he rang the little bell to tell the people in church that it was time for Holy Communion, his own heart filled with a deep joy. This was one of the days when he had received permission from the Prior to take Our Lord into his heart. Not every day, in Martin's time, could people receive Holy Communion.

"Lord, I am not worthy that Thou shouldst enter under my roof. Say only the word, and my soul shall be healed," he whispered, kneeling very still and straight before the golden altar that some rich Spaniard had given to the church.

If only people everywhere could understand the wonderful gift God had given them in the Holy Eucharist! There was not a man or woman in Lima who did not believe, when he or she was sick, that certain herbs and medicines could be of great use. But they did not seem to remember that sometimes

"LORD, I AM NOT WORTHY..."

the soul gets sick, too; that it becomes weak and tired and needs a medicine to make it as strong as it should be. If only people would take the medicine God offered them so freely, Martin thought— the wonderful Food and Drink that was Himself! After receiving Holy Communion, they could not help being stronger and better than before. Even if they didn't feel it, it was so.

"Come into my heart now, Lord," said Martin. "Be the medicine that my soul needs!"

Presently the Mass was over. Martin would have preferred to remain in the church, his face hidden in his hands, and his mind full of but one thing: *God was in his heart once more, making him strong and filling him with the desire to help all those who needed it.* But there was work to be done. He had the halls to sweep. There were tasks for him in the convent kitchen. The garden, where the Prior had given him leave to grow herbs for his medicines, had to be raked and weeded. There were three sick Brothers upstairs who would be wanting their breakfasts.

Knowing where his duty lay, Martin got up from his knees and followed the priest, whose Mass he had just served, into the convent cloister. Everything, even sweeping, scraping vegetables, weeding a garden and waiting on the sick could be a prayer, if it were offered to God. Quietly Martin once more gave his whole self and everything he would do that day to his Creator. He was only a poor Negro youth, whose race was looked down upon by the leaders of his country, but he knew that God is pleased with love. God will never turn away from any soul which lovingly gives itself and its work to Him.

Martin finished the duties indoors and went out into the garden. It was a beautiful day, the sun shining brightly on the long green rows of vegetables and herbs which he had planted a few months before. For a while he considered the scene before him. He was happy about this garden. The soil was good and everything was growing very well. The Prior himself admitted that Martin's garden was saving the convent a good deal of money, for it supplied fresh vegetables for the brethren, as well as the plants and shrubs whose juices could be made into medicine. And that was a good thing, for the convent was poor. Only recently the Father Prior had told the community that he owed quite a large sum of money, and Martin knew he was worried.

"I wonder what I could do to help," the boy thought, as he started to weed a long row of beans. "It must be such a worry that the convent is in debt."

So lost in thought was Martin about the problem at hand that he failed to see Brother Michael coming down the vegetable garden toward him. Brother Michael, the sacristan, was a lot older than Martin, and he had charge of the vestments the priests wore when they said Mass. He also looked after the candles for the altars and the bread and wine that were used at the Holy Sacrifice.

"Well!" said Brother Michael in a loud voice. "So this is where you are!"

With surprise Martin noted that Brother Michael

was carrying some linen altar cloths on his arm.
And he was looking very cross about something.

"Hello, Brother Michael!" cried Martin, straight-
ening up from his weeding. "Isn't this a lovely day?
And aren't the beans doing well?"

Brother Michael's mouth was grim. "*Beans?*" he
cried. "Who cares whether beans are doing well
or not? Just look at these altar cloths, Martin! What
are a few beans compared to them?"

Martin looked closely at the fine linen cloths.
"Why, they're full of holes," he said. "And all ragged
at the edges. How did that happen?"

"*You* should know," replied Brother Michael
stiffly. "The rats and mice are eating everything in
the sacristy. But they're not going to ruin any more
good altar cloths. I've just been to see Father Prior.
He told me to order you to get rid of the pesky
creatures at once. Every last one of them!"

Martin's heart fell. "Get rid of them? But how,
Brother Michael? Must I poison the poor little
things? They mean no harm. They don't know
about the value of linen..."

He broke off. It was clear that what he was saying
only sounded silly to Brother Michael, and was
making him still angrier.

"You heard what Father Prior said, Martin. Don't
argue with me." And with these words, Brother
Michael turned on his heel and went quickly out
of the garden.

Martin watched him go in great sadness. No
doubt it was all his fault that the good altar cloths
had been ruined. For years he had been feeding

the many dogs and cats that found their way into the monastery, leaving about scraps of food so that they would not starve. Why hadn't he thought to feed God's lesser creatures, too? The rats and mice? If only he had done this, the little things would never have feasted in Brother Michael's sacristy.

"How thoughtless I am!" he told himself. "The convent is in debt, and here I have caused Father Prior more expense. What can I do?" For somehow he felt responsible and it seemed unjust that the rats and mice should be killed. After all, is it a crime to eat when one is hungry? And yet the Prior had given an order. All the rats and mice were to be driven from the monastery. . .

It was as he was still weeding that a happy idea finally came to Martin. Perhaps the little creatures would not have to die after all, if they would just do what they were told. "I shall find a rat and tell him to call his brothers into the garden," Martin thought. "The same with the mice. Then I shall explain to them that they must eat no more linen in the convent. But I shall also tell them they will never lack for food if they will only stay in the barn. I shall feed them there myself, and pray that they keep out of mischief."

It was later in the morning that Martin saw a rat sitting under a berry bush, enjoying the sun. It was quite tame, and its bright eyes were friendly. Martin stood his rake against a tree and beckoned to the little creature.

"Come here, my little brother," he said. "I have something very important to tell you."

At once the rat pricked up its ears, then scampered joyfully toward him. As he knelt on the warm earth and thought of what to say, the sadness vanished from Martin's heart. He knew now, better than ever, that he loved every form of life that God had made.

"I want everyone and everything to be happy," he said. "Come here, little rat."

CHAPTER 7

VACATION IN THE COUNTRY

IN THE weeks that passed, everyone at Santo Domingo was amazed to find that the rats and mice really had obeyed Martin and no longer lived in the convent. Brother Michael, the sacristan, had no reason now to complain that the little creatures were eating his altar linens. They were living peacefully in the barn, and Martin fed them there every day.

"It's the strangest thing I ever heard," Brother Michael often told himself. "That Martin certainly has a way with animals. Who will ever forget how he spoke to that rat in the garden? In just a little while the message had gone to every rat and mouse in the place. I never could have believed it, if I hadn't seen with my own eyes how they came running out of their holes to follow their leader. There was a real army of them, marching out of the convent to the barn!"

But although the rats and mice no longer ate the linens in Brother Michael's sacristy, there were other troubles at Santo Domingo. The whole place was in debt, and the Prior had no idea where he was going to find the money he needed. Things kept going from bad to worse, and many were the prayers offered by those living at the monastery that God would soon see fit to help them.

"Why can't I think of something?" Martin asked himself over and over again. "The Fathers and Brothers have been so good to me all these years. It's only right that I should try to be of use to them when they are in trouble." But the days passed, and no ideas came to him. After all, what could he do to earn money? In the city of Lima, too many people thought that Negroes were good only to be slaves, to work for white masters until they died from hardship.

One morning Martin saw the Father Prior going out the gate. He was carrying some large pictures, and seemed to be heading for the marketplace. Martin stopped his sweeping for a moment to watch, and his heart ached for the poor Prior. The sun that lit up the rich gold frames around the pictures also revealed the tired lines in the gray-haired priest's face. Once more, Martin knew, the Father Prior was going out to try and sell some of the convent's valuables and thus get a little money to help pay off the debt.

"Oh, God! Give me an idea!" whispered Martin. "For nine years I've lived here at Santo Domingo, getting my food and clothes and shelter. Now, please let me help those who have helped me for so long!"

God must have heard this prayer, for suddenly a

bright idea popped into Martin's head. He would run after the Prior and offer himself to be sold instead of the pictures! He was young and strong. There were many rich people in Lima who would be glad to buy him for an extra Negro slave, and pay the Prior well. And as he stood there, with his broom in his hand, a great wave of longing arose in Martin's heart. How much better it was to do things for people, because God Himself loved them—and often even lived within them by Sanctifying Grace—than to be seeking one's own pleasure! How much better it was to give than to receive!

The Prior was very much surprised when, after going a few blocks, he found Martin at his side. The latter had run all the way from Santo Domingo and now was warm and breathless.

"Father, don't sell the pictures! *Please!* Sell me instead!"

The priest looked at the young man beside him. His heart was heavy with the worries of his office, but the burden lifted when he saw the love shining in Martin's eyes.

"Sell you, Martin?"

"Yes, Father. As a slave. Perhaps I would get a master who would really treat me as I deserve, who would make me work hard for him. At Santo Domingo I have really had too easy a time, and I know. . . ."

The Prior put a kindly hand on Martin's shoulder. "My son," he said, "who told you to do this?"

"No one, Father. I've been praying for so long that you would get the money for the debt, and since you didn't get it...well, Father, I'm pretty sure you can find someone who wants to buy me. Can't we go to the market now and look around?"

The Prior rested the heavy gold-framed picture against a nearby lamp post. He had always known Martin was good, kind and generous to everyone, but he had never dreamed he would go this far with his charity. Now he looked deep into Martin's eyes, and saw him in a new light. Martin's boyish eagerness to serve was hiding a great soul.

"Martin, we'll never be so poor at Santo Domingo that we'd want you to leave us. Never!"

"But Father, it's a way for you to get the money. . . ."

"There are some things that money can't buy, my son, and one of these is a faithful heart. Now go on home and don't worry any more about the debt. God will look after us all."

Martin nodded, although his heart was still troubled. His plan had seemed such a good one. Perhaps the Prior did not really understand how anxious the rich people in Lima were for young and strong Negro slaves. Perhaps, if he explained a little more. . . .But as Martin stood there on the street corner, busy with such thoughts, the Prior seemed to read his mind.

"No, my son. There's no need for you to tell me more. I understood quite well in the first place. But wait a minute...something's just occurred to me. . . ."

"Yes, Father?" said Martin hopefully.

"You've been with us nine years?"

"Yes, Father. I'm twenty-four years old now, and very strong and healthy. Suppose you let me be hired out to someone. . . ."

"My son, I've already told you what I think of that idea. No, it's occurred to me, Martin, that it's about time you had a little vacation. This afternoon I want you to get ready and go out to our country place in Limatambo. The change of air will do you good. Take two weeks to yourself, and don't worry about anything. Understand?"

Martin was taken by surprise, but the Prior refused to listen to any objections. With a hasty blessing, he was off down the street with his load of pictures. God willing, there would be someone to buy these from him at the market.

Martin returned to the convent, as he had been bidden, and that afternoon set out for the friars' country house in Limatambo. It was about ten miles from the city, a place where olive trees, cotton and sugar cane grew in great abundance. As the young man walked along the dusty road, he eyed the green landscape with satisfaction. How nice it was out here in the clean air, with the birds singing in the olive groves, the flowers blooming in the grass!

"But even though Father Prior wouldn't let me be a slave, I'm still going to pray that somehow he is able to pay the debt," Martin thought. "There are so many rich people in Lima. Surely one of them could help us a little."

When Martin was about two miles distant from the Dominican friars' property he spied three ragged little children playing by the roadside. They were Negroes, and probably their parents lived in one of the poor mud huts that studded the vast plain of Limatambo like mushrooms.

"Hello," he said, smiling at the children—two girls and a boy. "And how are you today?"

The girls stared at Martin shyly, but the boy decided not to be afraid. "We're hungry," he said. "Have you anything to eat?"

Martin looked at the basket on his arm. He had put a little bread and fruit in it just before leaving the convent, in case he should grow hungry on his long walk to Limatambo. Now he was hungry enough to eat something, but he knew he could have a good meal later on when he reached the friars' farm. On the other hand, the children's parents probably had very little to give them.

"I have some bread and some oranges," Martin said. "Would you like to help me eat them?"

The boy's face brightened. "Oh, can we really?" he cried. The little girls flashed friendly smiles at Martin. It was only too plain that now they would not be shy with him anymore.

Martin and the children, whose names were Pedro, Maria and Clara, sat down beside the road under an old palm tree that lifted its dusty green arms into the brilliant sunshine. The bread and oranges soon disappeared, in spite of the fact that Martin discovered he was not hungry after all.

"Don't leave a crumb," he told the children. "It's not right to waste the good things that God has given us."

"WHY ARE YOU WEARING CLOTHES
MADE OUT OF WHITE WOOL?"

At these words Pedro turned Martin's basket upside down. "There isn't one little crumb left," he said. "We were so hungry we ate up everything."

Six-year-old Maria, who had curly black hair that she wore in two little braids, climbed up on Martin's lap. "You're nice," she said. "Why are you wearing clothes made out of white wool?"

"Because I'm a Dominican, Maria."

"What's that?"

Martin smiled into the black eyes looking up into his own. "A Dominican, Maria? Why, a Dominican is a person who gives his life to God so that he may help himself and others to go to Heaven."

Clara's fingers touched Martin's sleeve. "But you're not a priest, are you?"

"No. And I'm not a Brother, either."

"What are you, then?"

"I'm a Tertiary. That's a person who belongs to the great religious family St. Dominic founded nearly four hundred years ago. St. Dominic was a wonderful man who loved God, and little children, too. Tell me, do you know anything about him?"

Pedro and the girls shook their heads. "Tell us about him," they begged. "And about God, too, Martin. We like to hear stories so much!"

Martin stayed two weeks at Limatambo. Even though he was on a vacation he kept busy. Each morning he went out into the fields, where the sun shone and the wind was cool and fresh, to work at the odd jobs he could find. One day he planted olive trees, another he went among the sheep and cattle and saw that they were in good health.

Because he knew all about medicine, it was not hard for him to treat the animals' cuts and sores. He did it so gently and so well that they were never afraid when they saw him, in his black and white habit, coming toward them.

"Certainly this young man is a wonder," said everyone at Limatambo. "We must ask the Prior at Santo Domingo to send him out here often."

But the two weeks were soon over, and Martin knew it was time to return home. He had loved his little holiday on the farm. It had been good to get out into the fresh air, to wander about the countryside visiting those who lived nearby. He knew every child now, and had passed many happy hours teaching them Catechism and telling them the thrilling stories of the Gospel.

"I shall come back," he told the boys and girls, whose faces were long and sad because they had just heard he was going home to Santo Domingo. "You wait and see. But there's one thing I'd like you to remember."

"I know!" cried Pedro. "Ask me, Martin!"

"Well? What is it?"

"You want us to remember that God loves us; that when we are good we are never alone, because He is living in our hearts."

Martin smiled. "But you're a little colored boy," he said. "Pedro, how can God be living in your heart when you are black?"

"Because He made me that way, Martin. He wanted some black and some white and some yellow and some. . .oh, He wanted different kinds of people on the earth, Martin, so He could have different kinds of places to stay! But He likes them all, as long as they are clean and nice for Him to live in."

Martin nodded. The children of the poor in Limatambo had learned one lesson anyway, a lesson which many of the world's great men and women would never understand.

CHAPTER 8

THE NEW LAY BROTHER

MARTIN HAD only been back at Santo Domingo a short time when the Prior gave him a piece of startling news. He, Martin de Porres, was not to be a servant in the convent any more. Instead, he was to be a lay Brother, a member of the First Order of St. Dominic.

"But I'm not worthy, Father Prior!" cried Martin. "I don't want such an honor. I just want to be useful, to work in the garden and the kitchen...."

"There's no use arguing, Martin. Everyone here thinks you should have been a lay Brother long ago. So, just to set your mind at rest, I'm going to *order* you to be one. There will be the usual ceremony and you can send word to your parents and your sister and any other friends who might like to come."

"Yes, Father Prior," said Martin.

For the rest of the day he could think of nothing else. He was to be a lay Brother! To make a solemn promise in front of many people that from now on he was especially God's own friend! And because of the solemn promise, every little thing he did, for the rest of his life, would have more merit in God's sight! Of course he knew his own good qualities. He knew that God had showered upon him many blessings. But these were only gifts, gifts to be used for God's glory and the salvation of souls. To God belonged the credit for any good he had done—to himself, only blame for not doing more. That is why he felt so unworthy of any honor.

But he couldn't argue now. The Prior had spoken, and he had to obey. At least his parents and his great-uncle up in Guayaquil would be happy about the new honor. And Jane, too. She had been married recently and was now living in Lima.

"God's Will, not mine, be done!" said Martin finally. "With His help I shall try to be a really good lay Brother."

Although he became a lay Brother, Martin's duties about the convent were still the same. He swept the halls; tended those who were sick; looked after the clothesroom; fed the poor and worked in the garden, raising vegetables for the kitchen and flowers for the different altars and shrines. Sometimes, under the warm sun, Martin thought how good it was to be busy, to have a chance to be useful to others. Our Lord, when He had lived on earth, had always been busy, not for Himself but for others. Now, though, how few people ever thought of the blessedness of work! They complained about their jobs. They dreamed of the day when they would have made enough money so that they could live in idleness. But Martin knew such thoughts were wrong. To work, when that work is offered to God in union with the merits of Christ, is one of the most wonderful things a person can hope for in this world.

One morning, as Martin was pruning some roses in the garden, he heard a great flapping of wings and a wounded bird fluttered helplessly to the ground. It made harsh little cries and its bright, beady eyes looked up at Martin as though to ask for help.

"My goodness!" cried the new lay Brother, dropping his pruning knife. "What can be the matter here?" And he bent down over the bird to find that one of its legs had been broken. Perhaps some boys had thrown a stone; or maybe some kind of trap had caused the injury. At once Martin began to set the bone and protect it with a splint.

"Brother bird," he said, "don't worry. You may live here in our garden until you are well. See that fountain? You will always find cool water there to drink. And I will bring you food myself."

The bird seemed to understand what Martin was saying. At least, it no longer seemed afraid, or in pain. But just as Martin was getting ready to start his pruning again, he saw a lame dog coming painfully toward him. The animal was dreadfully thin and his black coat was caked with dust and blood. At the pitiful sight Martin sighed. Here was still another of God's creatures in trouble.

"You were in a fight, weren't you, old fellow? Come here, and let me look at you."

The black dog came to Martin and put his head against the white habit. He was making sad little moans. "Well," said Martin, his gentle fingers parting the rough black hair, "you've been bitten by some other dog. And you've got a lame leg, too. What shall I do with you?"

The dog's soft brown eyes looked up at Martin pitifully, and the lay Brother laughed in spite of himself. "Don't look so sad," he said. "I'm sure things aren't that serious. But first we'd better wash that bite and get some ointment and a bandage to keep it clean. Come along, brother dog, and we'll see what we can do."

So Martin started off for the convent, the dog limping after him, and soon the two were in his bare little cell. In just a few minutes, the young man's skillful fingers had cleansed the wound and bandaged it. The black dog wagged his tail. He was already beginning to feel so much better.

"And now we'll see about that lame leg," said Martin. But even as he spoke, a bell rang in the distance. It was dinner time. The lay Brother patted the black dog's head.

"I'll have to go now," he said. "But don't worry. I'll be back. You just lie quietly on my bed and don't get into any trouble while I'm gone. Understand?"

The black dog's tail wagged again. He was only too happy to do what this kind young man told him.

Martin did not take very long eating his dinner. As soon as possible he left his place and went into the kitchen. There was a platter of vegetables on a table and a few loaves of bread in a wicker basket. He picked them up and started off toward the back door of the convent. It was just one o'clock. His friends, the poor, would be eager for this food. He must not keep them waiting.

There was a great shout of welcome as Martin appeared at the back gate. At least fifty men and women were waiting for him, and even some little children. Most of them were beggars, but Martin's quick eyes saw that a familiar little group was also present. These were servants whose masters were no longer rich, and who could not bring themselves to come in person for charity at Martin's hands.

"Brother, could I have a little bread?" cried one old woman, pushing her way to the front.

"Something for me!" begged a ragged little boy, pulling at Martin's habit with both hands.

"A little fruit, if you have it," one of the servants whispered in Martin's ear. "My good mistress is ill...although no one knows it...."

Martin smiled at the crowd. Then he spoke a few words over the platter of vegetables and the loaves of bread. Everyone there knew what those words were, for Martin never failed to say them:

"MAY THE LORD BLESS AND INCREASE THIS
FOOD, AND SATISFY ALL THOSE WHO COME."

For at least an hour, Martin stayed at the gate and gave out the food to the poor. A stranger might have been amazed that the vegetables on the platter and the loaves in the basket never seemed to grow any less, even though fifty hungry people ate their fill and gathered up what they wished to take home. But Martin never looked into his basket or at the platter to see how things were going. He acted as though there were no doubt that he had brought enough for everyone.

"Bless you, Brother Martin!" cried the crowd, when they had eaten all they could hold. "May you stay with us many years!"

Martin smiled. "Thank you, my friends. Don't forget the prayers you have promised to say for me."

There was still quite a little of the food left. Martin offered a quick little prayer of thanks to God for making possible such a wonder. Then, when the gate was shut, he turned his steps toward the barn. Here it was that others of his friends lived, the rats and mice who had once caused the sacristan such trouble by eating holes in the altar linens. But the little creatures had not entered the convent since the day when Martin had ordered them to stay away.

The barn smelled of fresh hay. Martin stepped inside with his vegetables and bread. There was a mother dog here with her puppies and a cat with her kittens.

"Here's your dinner, little friends," he called cheerfully.

At once a sleek gray cat left her kittens to come and purr at Martin's side, while a small white dog ran up to the plate which Martin was filling with vegetables. The lay Brother smiled to himself as both started to eat from the same dish. Dogs and cats were said to be natural enemies, but these two

"HERE'S YOUR DINNER, LITTLE FRIENDS."

were the best of friends.

He stood there for a moment watching, and thinking what a lesson men might learn from this picture. If dumb animals could learn to live peacefully together, why not the different races of the world? But he knew that this can only happen through God's grace, since only people in the state of Sanctifying Grace can love their neighbor the way God wants.

Then a little squeaking noise made Martin turn away for a moment. There, peeking out from a hole in the barn floor, was a tiny mouse. It was hungry and had smelled the food, but it was plain to see that it dared not come close to the dog and cat. Its bright eyes sought Martin's face, and the lay Brother stretched out his hand.

"Come on," he said kindly. "No one will hurt you."

The dog and cat stopped eating and made as though to chase the tiny creature back into its hole, but Martin shook his head. "Let the little thing alone. God made it, even as He made you and me."

Quietly then, he coaxed the little mouse toward the dish, and presently there were three animals happily eating the food which Martin had brought.

When Martin finally returned to his cell, the black dog was ready for his dinner, too. Martin fed him, attended to his lame leg, then brought him to the barn to join the other animals there.

CHAPTER 9

MARTIN AND HIS FRIENDS

THERE WAS another Dominican convent in Lima besides the one where Martin lived. It was about a mile away, and was dedicated to St. Mary Magdalen. Once a month Martin went there to visit his good friend, John Masias, a lay Brother like himself. Brother John was six years younger than Martin, and had left his native Spain for South America when he was only a boy in his teens. Like Martin, he had felt it his duty to enter the religious life, and so, shortly after arriving in Lima, he had asked to be a lay Brother in the Dominican convent of St. Mary Magdalen. The Prior was much impressed with the holiness of the newcomer, and had given him the task of feeding beggars at the gate and of greeting whoever should ring the bell at the convent's front door.

Martin was thinking about Brother John as he walked toward the convent of St. Mary Magdalen one sunny afternoon. It was his free day in the month. If he had wished, he could have gone to Limatambo with some of the other Brothers for a little picnic. But he usually chose to spend this free day in the city, talking and praying with Brother John Masias, or with another of his saintly friends, Brother John Gomez, who lived a few blocks away in the convent of St. Francis.

"I wonder what's happened to Brother John Masias since I was here last time," Martin thought. "I'm afraid he's wearing himself out with his penances and prayers."

He walked along quickly, turned the corner and went toward a heavy wooden door set in a high stone wall that ran the length of the street. There was a bell rope here. Martin pulled it, and almost at once a little window in the door opened and John Masias looked out.

"Praised be Jesus Christ," said Martin.

"For ever and ever. Amen," answered John. Then, with a smile: "Dear Brother Martin! How happy I am to see you!"

Martin stepped through the door. The high stone wall hid from view the beautiful garden of the convent. It also hid many other things, including the Christlike life of charity that was Brother John's.

"And I'm happy to be with you, Brother, for one more afternoon. You see, I've been worried about your health. Here, let me have a look at you."

Brother John smiled, and backed away. "Don't worry about me, Martin. I'm all right, thank God. And so is somebody else. Can you guess who?"

A faraway look came into Martin's dark eyes as he and his friend started to walk toward the back of the garden. "You mean Brother Louis? The one who cut his fingers?"

"That's right. The boy can't forget what you did for him the last time you came, Martin. His hand was so badly infected we were sure he was going to lose it. Yet after you fixed it for him..."

"Just a little healing powder, Brother John. Anyone could have done the same for the lad."

John Masias smiled. There was no use in arguing with Brother Martin de Porres. He would never take the credit for any of his good deeds. Yet when the time came for Brother Louis Guttierez to be ordained a priest, he could surely thank a Negro lay Brother that he had two good hands with which to offer the Holy Sacrifice of the Mass.

The sunny afternoon slipped away, as Martin and John visited together in a quiet corner of the convent garden. First they prayed. Then they talked— about God, about the needs of their own souls, about the missions in far-off lands, the poor and sick in the city of Lima. Like Martin, Brother John Masias fed the poor at his convent gate. Like Martin, he spent most of his time trying to bring happiness into lives that were sad and downcast. And like Martin, Brother John did everything for the love of God.

As the two sat quietly under a green palm tree, Martin looked at his friend. "How many people live here in your convent?" he asked suddenly.

"How many people? Over a hundred priests and Brothers."

"No one else?"

"About a dozen Tertiaries, I guess. Men who help

about the place in exchange for food and shelter. You were one of those once, Martin, over at Santo Domingo, until the Prior made you become a real religious."

"I know. But who else lives here, besides the priests and Brothers and Tertiaries?"

Brother John shook his head. "That's all. Unless you count the six orphan boys we picked up off the street last year. They don't have any real homes of their own, so the Prior keeps them with us."

Martin nodded slowly. "That's what I wanted to hear," he said. "About the six orphans. They are boys, I know. But what about girl orphans?"

"_Girl orphans?_ What makes you ask about them?"

Martin smiled. "My heart," he said. "Brother John, in our great city of Lima there are too few places where homeless children can stay. Some boys and girls are cared for in our convents of men and women, but that doesn't solve all the problem. It's harder on the girls, because they must have a dowry before they can be settled down in life. Since so many rich people have slaves, how are they going to be able to earn it? What's to become of these poor girls?"

John Masias shook his head. "Some of them die of hardship, I know. There are many others who slip into evil ways."

For a long time the two friends were silent. Martin was very busy thinking. In some ways it was a very good idea for a girl to have a dowry, a certain sum of money to help her furnish a home or to support her as a religious. But then again the custom was hard on poor girls. The religious societies in Lima did supply some with dowries, but Martin's heart bled for the others. What was to become of them?

Presently he turned to John Masias. "Maybe Don Mateo could help," he said. "He's been very generous whenever I've asked him for anything."

The latter nodded. "Don Mateo Pastor? Of course. He's the very man, Martin. Go and see him this afternoon, on your way back to Santo Domingo. We've both heard him say many times that God only gave him his wealth so that he could help those in trouble."

When Martin said good-bye to Brother John, the sun was beginning to set. There was no time to lose, if he wanted to lay his plan before Don Mateo and still be at the convent for supper.

"I just know Don Mateo will do something!" Martin thought as he hurried along the street. "He has a wonderfully kind heart. And his wife's a good soul, too. I remember her when she was a little girl. I lived with her mother, Doña Francisca Miquel, for a little while after I came back from Guayaquil. What a lot has happened since then!"

It was true. Martin had been a boy of ten years when he had left his great-uncle's house in Ecuador to come back to Lima to learn a trade. Now he was thirty-three. Many of his old friends were dead—his parents, Don Diego, Ventura de Luna, some of the priests and Brothers who had been so kind to him when he had first come to the monastery. Even his sister Jane had lost her first husband and now had taken another.

"They are the happy ones, the dead," Martin told himself. "They have begun the only life that matters."

So lost in his thoughts was Martin that he did not hear a boy's voice calling to him. Only when a pair of young hands suddenly clutched his habit and he found himself gazing down into the face of an Indian boy, did he realize that the youngster had been running after him for many blocks.

"Why, Anthony! What's the trouble? You're all out of breath!"

"Oh, Brother Martin! I thought I'd never make you hear!"

The lad's thin, dark face was anxious. "Please, Brother Martin, she's coming to see you about my mother. . .and the doctor says there isn't any hope. . .he says she's going to die. . .and leave me all alone! Oh, Brother Martin! You will come and pray, won't you?"

Martin put a kindly hand on the boy's shoulder. A stranger would not have known what the trembling lad meant, but he knew. *La Rosita*, who one day would be known as Saint Rose of Lima, was coming to Santo Domingo to ask his prayers for another poor invalid. *La Rosita* was a saint, as everyone in Lima knew, and she very often came to Santo Domingo to ask for prayers for the sick and homeless women she had taken into her father's house.

"Anthony, I'll come at once," he told the boy

cheerfully. "But here, you mustn't look so sad! Nothing's going to happen to your mother. She seems to be dying now, and she's having great pain, but tomorrow she'll be much better. You wait and see."

The Indian boy looked tearfully at the Negro lay Brother in his black and white habit. "How do you know?" he asked. "The doctor says. . ."

"Of course," replied Martin quickly, "but even doctors say one thing and God another, Anthony. Come along. We'll go and talk to *La Rosita* about your mother."

The two went hand in hand down the street. Before them loomed the tower of Santo Domingo. Martin smiled. He had thought to spend this hour before supper talking to his friend, Mateo Pastor, about the need for building an orphanage in Lima. But God willed otherwise. *La Rosita* was waiting for him, and this was a privilege for anyone.

When they reached the monastery, Martin sent his young companion into the church. "Say a few Hail Marys for your mother," he suggested. "I'll come and get you in a little while." Then he himself went into the visitors' parlor.

In the dimly lighted room, with its high carved ceiling, he saw *La Rosita,* "The Little Rose," waiting. He had known *La Rosita* for a long time now, and they had always had a great deal in common. As children they had both been baptized in the same church—San Sebastian. Today *La Rosita* was also a member of the Dominican Order, and wore the black and white habit of St. Dominic's family.

"WE'LL GO AND TALK TO *LA ROSITA*
ABOUT YOUR MOTHER."

Seven years younger than Martin, she had been famous throughout Lima ever since she had been a girl in her teens.

Scores of tales were told of her holiness: how she now lived in a little mud-brick house in her father's garden, and prayed for sinners night and day. Some said that hundreds of times she had seen and talked to her guardian angel and the Blessed Virgin. The Child Jesus, related others, often came and played games with her. At any rate, the young Dominican Tertiary was one of the most beautiful girls in Lima. If she had wished, she could have been a great lady in society. But Rose had never wanted to be anything but a saint; to pray and suffer for sinners was the life she had chosen.

"I met little Anthony just now," said Martin, crossing the room to where *La Rosita* stood waiting. "It's his mother, isn't it?"

The girl before him nodded. In the dim light she seemed younger than she was. Her hands held a well-arranged bouquet of blue and white flowers which Martin knew she had brought for the altar of Our Lady of the Most Holy Rosary. The dark eyes lifted to his own were alight with pity.

"The poor woman is in terrible pain, Brother Martin. I've done everything I can, and so has the doctor, but it isn't enough. I thought perhaps that you..."

She broke off and looked out into the cloister garden, with its blue and yellow tiled columns. Her parents and her brothers and sisters had little use for the poor beggar women she brought into the house from time to time. They were rather tired of seeing so many dismal creatures in their home. But Brother Martin—yes, he understood. He had never failed her yet. How many poor Indians and Spaniards had died with the Last Sacraments, had recovered their health, because of his good prayers?

"The doctor thinks the poor woman won't last through the night," she said softly. "Brother Martin, isn't there something we can do?"

With a tender smile Martin fingered the large wooden rosary hanging at his side. "Yes, little Rose, and you know what it is," he said gently. "We can keep on praying. We can keep on having faith. Hasn't that always worked in the past?"

CHAPTER 10

A BUSY DAY

THE SUN was high in the blue heavens as
Anthony, the Indian boy, came out of the
house of *La Rosita*. He had spent the night
here, close by his mother's side. Knowing how sick
she was, and that probably she would die before
morning, he had not been able to sleep. But now
the night was over, and his mother was still alive.
More than that, she was even beginning to feel
quite well. It seemed too good to be true.

"I must run and tell Brother Martin," the boy
thought, his heart singing within him. "Things have
turned out just the way he promised!"

The convent of Santo Domingo was not far away
from the low, rambling structure that was home to
La Rosita. Anthony covered the distance in just a
few minutes. But when he rang the bell at the convent, it was Brother Albert, not Brother Martin,
who answered.

"I'm sorry, lad," said Brother Albert. "Your friend
isn't here. I only wish he were, for old Brother
Thomas is dying upstairs."

At once some of Anthony's new-found happiness faded away. "But where is Brother Martin? I want to see him so much!"

Brother Albert shook his head. "He told me he was going to see his sister. But of course he'll do a dozen other things, too. He never wastes any time when he goes out. Only last week, when he came back from a walk, he had with him three sick Indians, a lost dog, an orphan boy and twenty loaves of bread. I tell you, life with Brother Martin de Porres is one long chain of surprises."

Anthony was disappointed at not being able to see his good friend, but he thanked Brother Albert just the same and was about to take his leave when the latter called to him.

"I almost forgot, lad. Brother Martin left something for you. He must have known you were coming. Here, in this package. . ."

Anthony's dark eyes widened. *"For me?"*

"For no one else. Open it up."

The boy undid the wrappings with excited fingers. "It's a pair of shoes!" he exclaimed. "And they're new ones! Oh, Brother Albert, I've never had new shoes in all my life!"

The latter smiled. "Somebody gave them to Brother Martin, I guess. You can come back this afternoon and tell him how they fit. He should be here by two o'clock."

Brother Albert was right. Promptly at two o'clock a black and white clad figure turned into the street where stood the Dominican church and convent. It was Martin, walking a bit slowly, for he was tired.

But there was a smile on Martin's face. An hour ago Don Mateo Pastor had promised to provide dowries for no less than twenty-seven poor girls who wanted to get married, as well as to do what he could about the orphanage for homeless children. Yes, Martin had had a very good visit with Don Mateo. And he had also had a nice time with Jane and her fourteen-year-old daughter, Catherine.

"My little niece is growing fast," he thought. And then he chuckled to himself as he recalled the request young Catherine had made of him that morning. It was not a doll she wanted this time. Or candy. It was a *mantilla*. It seemed that a *mantilla*, or lace veil, was very necessary if a girl was to look her best. No fashionable young lady in Lima ever went out without one of these fancy lace veils over her hair. And a big comb to hold it in place.

"Mother says she hasn't any money to spend on such foolishness," Catherine had told him. "She says I'm too young for a *mantilla*. But I'm not young, uncle Martin. I'm fourteen years old! And I do feel so awful not to be able to look as nice as the other girls. Can't you do *something?*"

Martin had smiled. Ever since he had been a little boy he had been doing what he could for God and for souls—and to make people happy. He had taught Catechism to small children. He had learned the secrets of medicine. He had cured hundreds of sick people. He had even found homes for stray animals. He had visited prisons and hospitals. He had fed and clothed countless beggars. Now he was to find a lace *mantilla* for his young niece, so she would not seem less well-dressed than her friends.

There was a broad smile on his face as he went up to the monastery gate and rang the bell. He would not disappoint Catherine. Not only would he send her a nice *mantilla*. He would send her half a dozen, so she could pick out the one that pleased her most.

It was Brother Albert who came to open the door, and his eyes lit up at the sight of the newcomer.

"Brother Martin! At last you're back! Oh, if you'd only come a bit sooner!"

Martin stepped inside. "Why, what's the trouble? Did someone want me?"

Brother Albert sighed, and made a very large and solemn Sign of the Cross. "Brother Thomas died an hour ago. Oh, Brother Martin! The poor old man called for you so many times! Why did you have to be away?"

Martin smiled. "I came as quickly as I could. But are you sure Brother Thomas is really dead?"

"Dead? Of course he's dead. They're getting ready to say the usual prayers right now. And, oh yes! Father Prior wants to see you at once. He's upstairs."

When Martin reached the second floor of the monastery, he saw that the Father Prior and many of the other priests and Brothers were assembled outside the door of the dead man's room. Each one had a large book containing the prayers they were about to say for Brother Thomas. As Martin came up the stairs, the Prior met him.

"He's been dead an hour, Brother Martin. You'd better get his body ready for burial. Find a new habit and put it on him."

Martin nodded silently and went into the little room. He knew there was a clean habit here for the dead man.

As the door closed, a strange silence descended over the little group of priests and Brothers standing in the hall. The first to speak was Father Andrew.

"Martin didn't seem very surprised at poor Brother Thomas' death," he said. "I wonder. . . ."

"What do you wonder?" asked the Prior.

"Haven't you noticed that Brother Martin always deals with sickness in a strange way? He never bothers with certain people, even when they're really ill. He seems to know they will be all right after a while. But there are other times when he will not go away from a sick bed. These cases are always the serious ones, even though they don't seem so to others. I was just wondering. . . since Martin wasn't here today. . ."

The little group was silent again, for Father Andrew's words had set them all to thinking. In the eighteen years that Martin de Porres had been living at Santo Domingo, a number of wonderful things had happened. It seemed quite certain, for instance, that many times God had given Martin the power which seemed to make it possible for him to be in two places at the same time. Strangers in Lima, who called at the monastery of Santo Domingo, insisted they had seen Brother Martin in

countries other than Peru. There had been one
man who had declared in a very loud voice that
Brother Martin had looked after him when he had
been a prisoner, and sick, in the Moorish city of
Algiers. There had been another, a sea captain, who
had sworn he had met Martin in China. Others had
said they had been looked after by Martin when
they were ill in Mexico, in Japan, in the Philippines.

At first everyone at Santo Domingo had been
inclined to laugh at these stories. Later, well...
they had not laughed. Martin was so good, so
wrapped up in Heaven and the doing of God's Will,
that it was very possible he might have been given
powers unknown to ordinary men.

"For eighteen years he has been here with us in
this monastery," said the Prior thoughtfully. "We
know that. And yet it is quite possible that God has
also let our Martin be in other places, too, to help
those in trouble. It is a gift given to a very few holy
people."

And as the priests and Brothers waited for the
door to open and the body of Brother Thomas to
be brought down to the chapel, they began to recall
other wonders in Martin's life.

"He passes through locked doors in the middle
of the night," said Father John. "He did it for me
once, when I was a young novice. I remember I was
very sick, and suffering from a high fever. Everyone
had gone to bed. I wanted a drink of water, but
there was no one to get it for me. My bed was
uncomfortable, too. Then I wished that Brother
Martin were with me. I knew he would make me

feel better. I closed my eyes for just a moment. When I opened them...why, there he was! With a drink of cold water in one hand and some fresh sheets in the other! And he would only smile when I asked him how he knew what I wanted, and how he had come through a locked door in the middle of the night."

Another priest, Father Philip, nodded. "Once he took several of us out for a picnic. It was a Holy Day, and we had been told that we might stay away from the monastery until six o'clock. We walked several miles into the country, and had a fine time with the good lunch Brother Martin had brought along. After we had eaten, we played games and told stories. Everyone forgot about the time. Then suddenly we looked at the sky. The sun had gone down and we were several miles from home. How were we going to get back in time for prayers at six o'clock?"

Father Andrew smiled. "I remember that day," he said. "I was Master of Novices then. But Brother Martin had you all back in plenty of time for prayers."

Father Philip nodded. "None of us ever knew how he did it," he said. "One minute we were in the country, worried about being late. The next, we were here at the monastery, on our way to the chapel with everyone else. It was a real miracle."

And so the priests and Brothers talked. One recalled how once the Rimac river was about to overflow its banks and flood a great part of the city. Martin had been called. Martin had prayed. And

HE HAD BEEN INSPIRED TO CALL THE DEAD MAN BY NAME.

at once the waters of the Rimac had started to go down. Another related how a month ago he had seen Martin praying before the large crucifix in the Chapter hall downstairs.

"I shall never forget that sight," he said. "Brother Martin was not on his knees. The power of God had lifted him from the floor to the side of Our Lord. And there he was, floating in the air and speaking to Christ on the cross. He must have been at least eight feet from the ground!"

As the little group continued to discuss the many wonders in Martin's life, the door to Brother Thomas' room suddenly opened and Brother Martin came up to the Prior.

"Everything's all right now," he said simply. "Brother Thomas wasn't dead after all."

The Prior stared. *"What?"*

Martin lowered his eyes. A little later he might try and explain to the Father Prior how he had prayed before the crucifix in the little room; how suddenly he had been inspired to call the dead man by name, and that, little by little, strength had come into Brother Thomas' cold body and he had opened his eyes. But not now would he tell the story. Perhaps Brother Ferdinand could do it for him. He had been in the little room, too.

Even as he spoke, Brother Ferdinand came into the hall. His face was white, his hands shaking. His eyes sought those of the Prior.

"Our Brother Thomas..." he said shakily, "he...he's having something to eat!"

CHAPTER 11

MARTIN'S YOUNG NEIGHBORS

TO MARTIN, the years at Santo Domingo seemed to fly. No doubt it was because he kept so busy. Sometimes, when he looked at the different priests saying their Office in the chapel, he sighed. They had been but boys yesterday, boys coming to offer their lives to God in the Order of St. Dominic. Now they were grown men, some of them famous throughout Peru for their great learning.

"Help them to bring many people to know You," Martin would pray. "After all, that's the most important thing in life: to think about You a lot, to come to know how good You are, and then to love You more than anyone or anything."

Martin often had such thoughts. He did not read difficult books. He had only had two years of schooling. Yet everyone at Santo Domingo knew he was a wise man. He could think straight. He knew how to be honest with himself, and with others. Young students for the priesthood often came to him with their problems. They all knew the Negro lay Brother, whose black hair was now starting to be flecked with white. When they became ill, it was he who looked after them. When they needed something, for themselves or their families, it was Martin who always came to the rescue. And when a few of them became lonesome at Santo Domingo, and feared they could never lead the life of a Dominican priest or lay Brother, Martin was always on hand with a word of encouragement.

One late afternoon a few of the novices came to Martin's cell. For a wonder, no sick Indian or Negro was lying on his bed. The little room was empty.

"Martin must have gone out for a while," young Brother Jerome said to his friends. "But didn't he promise us a lunch today, after our classes were over?"

"I heard him with my own ears," said Brother Charles. "He said: 'Boys, after your last class is over, go to my room. I'll have a little lunch ready for you.' Well, where's the lunch?"

Martin's room was very small. There was nothing in it but a bed, chair and table. For a while the students sat on the bed and amused themselves, but suddenly one of them had a bright idea.

"Maybe Martin left something for us in the table drawer," he said. "Let's have a look."

When he pulled open the drawer and found several apples and oranges, there was a great shout of joy, for everyone was very hungry and the fruit looked good.

"Martin wouldn't mind if we helped ourselves," said Brother Jerome. "Come on, everybody. There's plenty to go around."

The novices went over to the table and took what they wanted from the drawer, an apple for this one, an orange for that. There was much talking and laughing in the little room. In the excitement, no one noticed that one of the novices had quietly put his hand far back in the drawer, taken something from it very quickly, then hidden it in his shoe. When the door suddenly opened and Brother Martin came in, there was a general shout of welcome.

"We've helped ourselves to your fruit," said Brother Edward. "We hope you don't mind, Martin. We were awfully hungry."

Martin smiled. "I left it there for you boys. Take all you want. And I've brought you some bread and honey, too. While you eat, I'll just sit here on the floor and watch."

The little party in Martin's room was a big success, and all too soon the bell rang to call the community to prayers. At once the novices got up to go, but Martin held out his hand.

"Just a minute, boys. One of you has taken something that doesn't belong to him—a silver coin."

The novices stared at Brother Martin. "Why, that's impossible," said one of them. "We never saw any money here."

The little room was suddenly quiet. Martin waited a moment, then went over to one of the boys. "Give me the little coin you took, Brother," he said kindly. "It doesn't belong to you, or to me. It has an owner."

The young man flushed. "I don't know what

you're talking about. I never took any money."

Martin looked at him calmly, then pointed to his shoe. "Take it out of there," he said gently. "There is a cross on that little coin. It doesn't fit well down there, Brother, the sign of our holy Faith."

The other novices were silent. They could hardly believe their eyes as they saw the young Brother slowly put his finger into his shoe and bring out the missing coin. Then it was true after all! But how had Brother Martin known? He hadn't been in the room when the money had been taken.

"I guess you can't fool Martin," whispered Brother Jerome, as they went downstairs to the chapel. "It must be right what they say about him—that he can read people's souls."

When the novices had gone to the chapel, Martin stood for a long time looking out of the window. He was tired today. When he was younger, he had been able to walk long distances, to spend hours with the poor and sick, and never mind it. But now the ten mile walk to the harbor town of Callao was possibly too much for him. He had been there and back today, with food for the needy folk living along the waterfront. Early in the morning he had given away his straw hat to a poor man. It wasn't a very good hat, but he had missed it after a while. The sun had been very hot.

With a little sigh, Martin got down on his knees before the crucifix that hung over his bed. He had an hour or so before supper. He would spend it in prayer. Very rapidly his thoughts turned to Heaven. Perhaps it would not be so long before God, in His

"TAKE IT OUT OF THERE," HE SAID GENTLY.

goodness, would call him to enjoy the wonderful things He had planned for all those who serve Him faithfully. For many years now his little friend, *La Rosita*, had been in Heaven. There were others, too. The famous Franciscan priest, Father Francis of Solano, who had made the city of Lima resound to his mission sermons...the good Archbishop Turribius, who had given him the Sacrament of Confirmation...oh, it would be good to meet all these holy citizens of Lima someday, to enjoy with them the beauties of Paradise!

Time passed. Martin never noticed how the night came on, how the hall outside his room echoed to the sound of passing feet. Even when everyone at Santo Domingo had finally gone to bed, Martin still knelt in prayer. He had forgotten his aches and pains. He had forgotten everything but the one love of his life—God!

Early the next morning a fourteen-year-old Spanish boy stood before Brother Ferdinand in the clothesroom of the monastery. His name was John Vasquez, and he had only recently come to live at Santo Domingo. He was a stranger in Lima, without friends or money, and Martin had given him leave to sleep in his room until he could find a job. John was busy now, trying to tell a story to Brother Ferdinand about his good friend, Martin de Porres.

"I went into his room last night, at midnight, Brother Ferdinand. The big earthquake was going on, as you know. I was terribly scared. But it was worse, when I saw him..."

Brother Ferdinand busied himself sorting out the

clean linen. "You'll soon learn not to be surprised at anything about Brother Martin," he said. "What was the good soul doing?"

"He was lying on the floor. And though it was midnight, his cell was bright as day. I pulled and tugged at him to come with me, but he would not move. I...I thought he was dead. Oh, Brother Ferdinand, I thought the earthquake had killed him! And he's my very best friend in the whole world!"

Brother Ferdinand smiled. "If you live here long enough, you'll know better than to be frightened when you see Martin lying on the floor like that," he said. "Why, I have seen him...now listen well, lad...I have seen him flashing through the halls like a ball of fire."

"*A ball of fire?*"

"That's right. He was carried swiftly through the air, and light shone from him. And there are some people here who have seen him walking about the place with four angels to keep him company."

Young John shook his head. "I never met such a wonderful man as Brother Martin," he said slowly. "He's so kind and understanding."

Brother Ferdinand nodded. "You're not the only one to think so. Everyone loves him, although it's the young people he cares for especially. The novices are always coming to him for help in their studies. Of course, Brother Martin never had much schooling. But he can always help the students with their problems. It's simply wonderful the way he can quote from the Bible. He even knows all about the writings of St. Thomas Aquinas!"

John sat down on a stool beside Brother Ferdinand. "Brother Martin says I can help him look after the poor. He's been giving me money every day to take around to different poor families. Sometimes the two of us give out as much as two thousand dollars in one week. Where does he get all that money, Brother Ferdinand?"

"Martin? Ah, you'd be surprised how many wealthy people he knows. Even the Governor gives him money for his charity. Then Martin gets blankets for poor Indians, medicines for the sick, dowries for girls, clothes for babies...oh, there's no end to what he does with the money people give him!"

John nodded. He was a newcomer to Santo Domingo, but already he knew that Brother Martin de Porres was the best friend anybody could have. It was a pleasure to know that in a few minutes the door to the clothesroom would open and the lay Brother would appear, ready to take him on another day's trip among the city's needy.

Martin was on his way to the clothesroom to meet young John Vasquez. They had a lot to do today, for after they had given out the usual amount of food and money to the poor, they were going out to the hills above the city to plant some herbs and fig trees. But just as he was nearing the clothesroom, something stopped Martin. It was the sight of several ragged Indians sweeping up a small hallway. Brother Dominic was watching over them with a keen eye, and Martin could see that the Indians were being made to do a good job.

"Why, where did all these good people come from, Brother Dominic? Why are they sweeping the hall?"

Brother Dominic scowled. "I've just given them a good meal," he said. "It's only right that they should clean up the crumbs and leave the place · looking neat."

Martin smiled. "I saw you feed some white men yesterday," he said. "You didn't make them clean up afterwards. You did it yourself."

Brother Dominic shrugged his shoulders. "I don't mind cleaning up after white men, but to clean up after Indians? Well, Brother Martin, I guess that's just a little bit too much."

"Why?" said Martin gently.

"Why? Because it just doesn't seem right."

"Why?" said Martin again.

Brother Dominic, who was really a good man, suddenly seemed a bit confused. He couldn't answer the question. After all, when one looked at things squarely, a man was a man, no matter to what race he belonged. Why hadn't he thought of that before? He stammered something to Martin and walked over to the Indians, who were still sweeping the floor.

"That's enough," he said quickly. "I'll finish the job myself."

Watching him, Martin smiled. How much sadness was caused in the world because millions of people, even very good people, forgot that all men were made by God and redeemed by the Precious Blood of Christ!

CHAPTER 12

MARTIN TAKES A REST

MARTIN HAD lived at Santo Domingo for forty-five years, and there was hardly anyone in Lima who did not know him. He had made little children happy; he had found husbands for poor girls without any money; he had helped other young people to become priests and nuns; he had settled quarrels, fed the hungry and cured thousands of sick people. And whenever Martin cared for bodily needs, he was thinking even more of the soul inside. He knew that the most important thing for anyone was to have a soul bright and beautiful with Sanctifying Grace.

Most of the sick people Martin cured had been poor, but Martin also had been called frequently to the homes of the wealthy. He had cured Don Juan de Figueroa, a councilman of Lima, of a serious illness. He had also restored to health the Archbishop of Mexico, Don Felician de Vega, when the latter had fallen sick on a visit to Lima.

One day Father Cyprian de Medina, after looking all through the convent, found Martin sweeping in the kitchen. Father Cyprian was a nephew of the Mexican Archbishop, and as he hurried up to the lay Brother, he could hardly control his excitement.

"Brother Martin! I have a big surprise for you! You're going to go to Mexico with His Grace, my uncle!"

Martin smiled at Father Cyprian. How well he remembered those days, so many years ago, when this same priest had been an awkward young novice. How people had laughed at him then, because he was so clumsy! Now he was a famous scholar, a fine-looking man, and a credit to the Order.

Martin stopped his sweeping for a moment. "Mexico, Father Cyprian? Why ever should I go there?"

Father Cyprian chuckled. "You're not fooling me," he said. "You know as well as I do that my uncle wants to have you live with him. He says you're a treasure. Only recently you saved his life, and he doesn't want to let you out of his sight."

Martin sighed. No matter what he said or did, no one ever seemed to believe that the thousands of cures that had happened at his hands were not his doing at all. They were the work of God, in answer to a simple prayer.

"His Grace, the Archbishop, would have recovered without my help," he said. "Dear Father Cyprian, why are you always trying to make me feel proud?"

The priest flung up his hands. "What an impossible man you are!" he cried. "Brother Martin, have you forgotten what you did for me? How I was once

MARTIN HELD TIGHT TO HIS BROOM.

the laughing-stock of the convent because of my looks? How I was too short and too fat. . . ."

"You always had a good heart, Father Cyprian."

"How I was stupid at books? How I was never able to. . ."

"God was always your only love, Father."

"How you prayed for me when I fell sick as a novice, and afterwards no one recognized me because I had grown twelve inches, become a good student and changed in all my looks? Ah, dear Brother Martin! Where would I be without you?"

"Here at Santo Domingo," smiled Martin, smoothing the handle of his broom.

But even as he stood there, smiling at Father Cyprian, a familiar pain stabbed his whole body with the suddenness of lightning. Of late, it had been with him often, that pain. Was this the reason that he could smile at Father Cyprian's bit of news that the Archbishop wanted to take him to Mexico? In his heart, Martin knew that soon God would be calling him to go on another and much more important journey. It was to be in Heaven, not Mexico, that he would make his home.

Father Cyprian seemed to sense that something was wrong, and that strange thoughts were passing through his friend's mind. "You're ill!" he cried anxiously. "Brother Martin, why didn't you tell me? Why aren't you in bed, instead of working here in the kitchen?"

Martin held tight to his broom, hoping that the familiar, sharp pain would pass away. "I'm all right," he managed to say. "It's only natural for an old man to feel his age now and then."

The priest peered anxiously into Martin's eyes. "Sixty years isn't so old," he said, but his face wore a worried look just the same. How dreadful if anything should happen to Brother Martin!

"You go and lie down for a while," he said. "You've been working too hard. I'm going to tell the Prior so right now."

Martin smiled. "All right," he said. "But first I'd like to finish this sweeping."

It was only a few days later that the priests and Brothers at Santo Domingo were surprised to see Martin wearing a brand-new habit. Not one of them could remember such a thing ever happening before. Always the poorest and most patched habits had been Martin's choice.

"What's ever come over him?" they asked one another. One priest, Father John de Barbaran, jokingly spoke to Martin about his fine new attire.

"What's this, Brother?" he asked. "Are you suddenly becoming vain about your clothes?"

Martin shook his head. "No, Father. I just want to have a new habit for my burial."

Father John stared. "*Burial?* Why, Martin! What do you mean?"

"I mean I'm going to die, Father. In about four days."

The whole of Santo Domingo was in an uproar when the news broke. Brother Martin de Porres, who had been right about so many things in the past, had now announced that he was going to die; he had said there was no use in calling a doctor because his time on earth was up.

"It can't be true!" cried Father Cyprian.

"We mustn't let it happen!" exclaimed the Archbishop of Mexico.

"Spare no expense to save him!" begged the Viceroy. But Martin just smiled, and quietly one night, still wearing his new habit, he went to his cell and lay down upon his bed.

"My time has come," he thought. "Soon the only life that matters will begin for me."

When the news of Martin's approaching death leaked out, the people of Lima came rushing to Santo Domingo. Indians, Spaniards, Negroes, all the men and women whom the lay Brother had ever befriended had the same idea—they wanted to see their good friend once more. The Viceroy himself, Don Luis Fernandez Bobadilla, arrived in his golden carriage to speak with Martin and to ask his prayers.

"I'll only stay a minute," Don Luis told the Prior. "I don't want to tire my good friend. But is it true what people are saying? Is Brother Martin really going to die?"

The Prior shook his head. "Brother Martin has but a few hours more, Your Excellency. Come, I'll take you to him."

The two men, one in the black and white habit of the Dominican Order, the other in his royal robes of office, went slowly through the corridors to Martin's cell. On the way a young novice met them. His hands were trembling, and there was a frightened look on his pale face.

"Father Prior, Brother Martin doesn't want to see any visitors now. He...he told me to tell you!"

The Prior looked surprised. "But His Excellency is here, my son. Tell Brother Martin to get ready to see Don Luis."

In obedience the young novice bowed his head, but the Viceroy, representative of the King of Spain in Peru, put a kindly hand upon his shoulder. "What's the trouble?" he asked gently. "You're shaking like a leaf."

The young man raised his eyes. "Your Excellency, I did not know our Brother Martin was so...so *holy!* Just now I saw him, and he was talking...as though there were people in the room...as though St. Dominic and the Blessed Mother were with him...helping him not to be afraid of death! Oh, it was like a miracle!"

The Prior made an impatient move, but Don Luis stopped him. "Let's wait until the good Brother sends for us," he said humbly. "Truly, he is now with better company than ours."

Fifteen minutes passed, and then a lay Brother came quickly through the corridor to where the Prior, the Viceroy and the young novice were waiting. He, too, was shaken with emotion.

"Brother Martin is ready now," he said. So, with the Prior at its head, the little company once again started off toward Martin's cell.

Inside the tiny room, the Negro lay Brother lay quietly on his bed, a crucifix in his work-worn hands. His dark eyes were very bright. Don Luis, despite his rich clothes and high rank, fell upon his knees beside his dying friend.

"Brother Martin, you'll not forget me when you go to Heaven? You'll still pray for me, that I fulfill my duties well?"

Martin nodded. The pain was getting worse now. He could scarcely see the face of the Viceroy, or that of the Prior. But he could see other faces— beautiful, radiant—that seemed to smile upon him and bid him not to be afraid. Was that not the Blessed Mother, stretching out her hands to him? Was that not his patron and father, St. Dominic? His brother and friend, St. Vincent Ferrer?

"I shall never forget you, Your Excellency," he murmured. "In Heaven I shall pray God to bless you, and all my other friends."

Slowly the hours passed. Darkness descended upon the royal city of Lima, and one by one the lights came on in the palaces of the rich, the hovels of the poor. Martin stirred uneasily. He was very tired now, for all day the Devil had been trying to make him afraid of death. But he could still hope in God's mercy.

In a corner of the room he could hear the convent's physician, Don Francisco Navarro, preparing still another medicine. A little smile flickered over Martin's face. "Please don't bother," he whispered. "This is the end, and nothing can save me."

The Prior bent over the bed. He had been a little displeased that afternoon when Martin had sent word that he did not wish to see the Viceroy at once. Now, however, he knew the real reason, and his whole soul marveled.

"Shall I call the others, Martin?" he asked gently. "Shall we start the community prayers?"

The dying man raised his eyes to the Prior's face. It seemed but yesterday that he had come to Santo Domingo, a boy of fifteen, to serve the priests and Brothers. Now that service was almost done. How brief was even the longest life in which to work for God and earn the chance to be with Him forever!

"I have only a few minutes more," he whispered. "Yes, call the others, Father."

It was half-past eight. Slowly the great bell in the tower began to ring, the deep solemn peals that told of approaching death. Martin clutched his crucifix in damp fingers. All about him were flickering wax tapers. In his ears were the sounds of many voices, the rustle of rosaries, the tread of hurrying feet. His friends and brothers in St. Dominic's family were coming to be with him in these last moments.

Quietly he closed his eyes. Familiar words were in his ears now. *"God of God...Light of Light...Who for us men, and for our salvation, came down from Heaven and was incarnate by the Holy Ghost...of the Virgin Mary...* AND WAS MADE MAN..."

With a happy sigh, Martin's fingers loosened about his crucifix. His days of struggle were over at last.

CHAPTER 13

HERO IN BLACK AND WHITE

ALL NIGHT long the priests and Brothers at Santo Domingo watched by Martin's body. As the cold dawn finally broke over the city, and the news crept from house to house that Martin had gone home to God, the streets were filled with hundreds of people hurrying to the Dominican church. The doors were not yet open, and as he paced up and down the aisle where Martin's body lay awaiting burial, Father Cyprian de Medina listened to the murmur of the huge crowds outside. He had not slept all night, and now his face was drawn and pale.

"Martin, what are we going to do without you?" he thought, and for the hundredth time he knelt down to pray beside the cold and lifeless body of his friend. But for hours now all words had stuck in his throat. It seemed like some horrible dream that the lay Brother whom he loved had gone from him forever. How could he pray, when sorrow was cutting into his heart like a sharp knife?

"Martin, why are you lying there so cold and

111

stiff?" he moaned. "Why can't you make something
wonderful happen to let us know you have really
gone to Heaven? To cheer our hearts and
strengthen our faith?"

Even as he spoke, he stretched forth his hand
and placed it upon Martin's body. The flesh was icy
in death. The fingers, holding a crucifix, were stiff
as wire.

"I want a miracle, Martin," whispered Father
Cyprian earnestly. "And so does everyone else.
Don't just lie here, like any other dead man. Do
something, won't you?"

The others watching felt sorry for Father
Cyprian. He was taking Martin's death very hard.
Yet it was only natural. Hadn't the two always been
the closest friends? Hadn't it been Martin's prayers
that had changed Father Cyprian from a dull, awkward novice into a fine-looking, clever priest?

"Perhaps something will happen," they thought.
"Perhaps Martin will work a miracle or two, if we
only give him time."

Fifteen minutes passed. Father Cyprian still
knelt beside the body of his friend. The murmur
of the great crowd at the church doors was louder
now. Brother Martin's friends were growing impatient at being kept outside. Father Cyprian listened,
then looked once again at his friend. Was it possible
that, in the flicker of the wax candles, Brother Martin's face was now more lifelike than it had been?
That now it even had a little color? Hopefully, the
priest stretched out his hand to touch his friend
once more, and almost immediately his heart gave

a great leap of joy. The body was warm! The fingers were no longer stiff!

"Oh, Martin!" cried Father Cyprian, sudden tears of joy streaming down his face. "You've done it after all! You've given us a sign that you're with God, and that He wants the whole world to know it!"

The sorrow which had prevailed all night in Santo Domingo speedily gave place to joy. The doors of the church were thrown open and immediately the impatient citizens of Lima surged up the aisles to see for themselves the wonder that had just happened. All day long men, women and children pressed forward to catch a glimpse of their beloved friend. Some had brought rosaries and medals that they wanted to touch to the holy body. Others had scissors with which they quietly snipped little bits from the black and white habit. Very soon the new habit which Martin had taken for his burial was no longer fit to be seen. Everyone, it seemed, wanted a relic, and from time to time another habit had to be brought from the convent and placed upon Martin's body.

"This can't go on," announced the Prior finally. "As fast as we clothe the body with a new habit, people keep cutting it up."

"But it's only because they know our Martin is a saint," the other religious reminded him. "Everyone wants a relic so they can remember him, and to have as a cure against future illness. Oh, Father Prior, can you blame them?"

After a moment's hesitation, the Prior spoke.

"No, I can't," he said. "And, with all these crowds, it even looks as though we might have to postpone the funeral."

It was true. So many people had flocked to see Martin's body (which now was warm and soft like that of a living person) that the funeral was put off until the next morning. In her heart, one woman gave thanks to God for this delay. She was Doña Catherine Gonzalez, of noble Spanish birth, and for twelve years she had not been able to use one of her arms. To make matters worse, it pained her all the time.

"Brother Martin could cure me if he wanted to," she thought. "Perhaps if I go over to Santo Domingo, and touch his body. . ."

So Doña Catherine called her nine-year-old son, whose name was Francis, and Doña Jacoba, who was one of her friends, and got ready to go to the Dominican church. All the way over, young Francis was very excited.

"Is Brother Martin going to cure your arm, Mother? Is he really going to make you well?" the boy kept asking.

Doña Catherine nodded, although she could not bring herself to say how really weak her faith was. One minute she believed that Martin would help her. The next, she wondered if he really would. After all, the Dominican lay Brother had worked most of his miracles for the poor. Would he bother with her, who was of noble and wealthy birth?

Suddenly she reached down for her little son's hand. "We must try to believe in Brother Martin's good heart," she said, her voice shaking a little. "Even if it is hard, we must try to have faith, Francis."

When Doña Catherine and her little party reached Santo Domingo, they found the streets about the church jammed with people. A peculiar fragrance, like that of lilies, hung upon the air. They joined the crowds that were slowly edging into the church, all the time sensing that strange sweet smell as of many flowers.

"What is it?" Doña Catherine asked an old woman beside her.

"I have never known any perfume like this," said Doña Jacoba.

"It's awfully good," said little Francis, wrinkling up his nose.

The old woman looked at Doña Catherine and Doña Jacoba. She was poor and ragged, while everything about the other two women and the little boy told of luxury. But it was the same thing that was bringing them all to Santo Domingo. Each of them wanted to see Martin's body before it was buried, to pray before it and to ask for the things they needed.

"They say it is a sign from Heaven, this perfume," she answered. "It has been all about Brother Martin's body for hours. That only happens to saints, I think."

Doña Catherine nodded. "He must have been a wonderful person," she said. "We have come here to ask God, in his name, for my health. Do you think he will hear us?"

The ragged old woman smiled. "I knew Brother Martin well," she said. "I never saw him turn down anyone who asked his help."

It took Doña Catherine over an hour to get inside the church, and then she saw a sight she would never forget as long as she lived. People of all races and colors were packed in the aisles on their way to pay tribute to the dead Negro lay Brother. Doña Catherine's heart beat fast as she and the people pressing about her slowly came to the place where Martin's body was lying. Was it really true, as the old woman had said, that Brother Martin always helped those who asked his aid?

"Oh, give me faith!" she whispered. "Dear God, let Brother Martin be made more glorious than ever by showing his power through me!"

Little Francis stared wide-eyed at Martin's body, lying so calm and peaceful in the light of the tall wax candles. It was the first time he had ever seen a dead person.

"But I'm not afraid of you, Martin," he whispered, while all about him the grown people pushed forward to get a better view. "Why should I be? You're going to make my mother's arm well!"

At last it was Doña Catherine's turn to kneel briefly beside Martin's body. Doña Jacoba knelt with her, and Francis, too. All three kissed Martin's hand and begged him to work just one more miracle before he was buried.

"Why don't you take his hand and rub it on your arm?" whispered Doña Jacoba. "Here, let me roll up your sleeve. They won't let us stay long,

Catherine, so we'd better pray as we've never prayed before!"

Doña Catherine knelt a moment with Martin's warm black hands in hers, the same hands that so often had blessed the sick and given food to the hungry. Then she got to her feet.

"Let's go over to the side aisle," she whispered. "Come, Francis. We mustn't get in the way of the others who want to say a little prayer."

Doña Catherine, with Doña Jacoba and Francis, made their way over to the side of the church. As they pushed through the crowds, they heard the sound of bitter weeping. Turning, they saw it was a Negro woman with a heavy black veil over her head. She was standing by the wall with some friends, and they were trying to comfort her.

"Poor soul!" whispered a voice behind them. "It's Jane de Porres, Brother Martin's sister. I guess she feels pretty bad."

For a moment Francis looked at the weeping woman. Then he seized his mother's good arm. "Did Martin cure you, Mother? Did he make your arm well?"

"Sssh!" whispered Doña Jacoba, as a few people turned to smile at the excited child. "We'll find out in just a minute. Here, Catherine. Let me take a look."

Doña Catherine never said a word. She knew, without rolling up her sleeve a second time, that her useless arm was now quite well. For the first time in twelve long years it did not pain. Now she could feel the blood rushing into the fingers that had been so limp and dead. Now she could feel the power in her muscles, the strength suddenly in the hand that had been useless for so long.

"He heard me," she said in a low voice that somehow she could not feel was her own. "Brother Martin heard me, just as he always hears the prayers of everyone in trouble!"

Doña Jacoba rolled up her friend's sleeve. The withered arm was now firm and strong. "God be praised!" she cried, and fell upon her knees. And then, she and Doña Catherine burst into joyful tears. Nine-year-old Francis could not understand.

"Don't cry, Mother," he begged. "Don't cry, Doña Jacoba."

Doña Catherine quickly whispered, "I'm so happy, my son! Martin has heard my prayer. My arm is cured!"

For hours the people continued to file into the Dominican church, to marvel at the sweet fragrance that hung upon the air, to hear about the wonderful cure of Doña Catherine Gonzalez. Finally, however, the Prior gave word that the funeral had been put off long enough and now must be held. Four lay Brothers were given the task of carrying Martin's body to the vault under the Chapter hall, where it was to be laid in a section especially reserved for the priests of the convent of Santo Domingo.

"In life, our Martin considered himself only a servant," the Prior said, "but in death we can pay him a little honor. He has brought glory to our land of Peru, and to our city of Lima, even as *La Rosita,* our holy Archbishop Turribius, and the good missionary priest, Father Francis of Solano. Someday his story will be known all over the world, and every race will call him friend."

However, when the four lay Brothers came to carry the body into the convent for burial, they found four other men who insisted on having the honor instead. One of these was the Archbishop of Mexico, who only recently had wanted to take Martin home with him. The second was the Viceroy, Don Luis Fernandez de Bobadilla. The third was Don Pedro de Ortega, a holy man who one day would be Bishop of Cuzco. The fourth was Don Juan de Peñafiel, a judge of the Royal Court. Everyone was astounded that such important men should wish to be pallbearers at a poor Negro's funeral.

"Your Excellencies," said the astonished Prior, "there is really no need for you to carry Martin's body to the grave. We had already arranged that four lay Brothers..."

"A chance like this comes only once in a lifetime," said the Archbishop of Mexico. "Father Prior, we think it an honor to do this little service for our good Brother Martin."

What could the Prior say? He nodded his head in agreement, and slowly the funeral procession got underway. It was November 5, in the year 1639. Forty-five years before, a Negro boy of fifteen had come to Santo Domingo to offer his life to God. He was a member of a race that many people despised, yet so strong had been his love for souls that he was now among the heroes of his native city.

"Perhaps among the heroes of the world," thought the Prior. And, as he followed in the funeral procession, he knew one thing: Martin de Porres would always live in the hearts of Catholics. His body would soon be in a grave, but his soul was in Heaven forever. It was a strong, bright and loving soul that, all through the centuries, would never turn away from those who asked for help.

Slowly, very slowly, the four pallbearers carried Martin's body out of the church. As the doors into the cloister opened, the crowds streamed through to have a last look at their good friend. Although it was against the rule for women to enter here, there was no use in trying to keep them out today. Their love for Brother Martin was too great.

Quietly the procession moved past the garden, past the blue and yellow tiled columns of the cloister walks, the fountain, the gay flowers that Martin had loved, into the convent. The crowds still pressed after the body, and as they came to the Chapter hall, their eyes lifted to the wall where hung the great crucifix which had spoken to Martin so many times. Night after night, for many years, the Negro lay Brother had prayed in this room while other people slept. Here the power of God had lifted him to the side of the wounded Christ. Here he had told Our Lord of the sorrows of his friends and of his own love. Now he was about to be buried in the vault under the floor.

"Brother Martin, do not forget us!" sobbed a woman's voice. "Help us to go to Heaven, too!"

EVERY RACE WILL CALL HIM FRIEND.

The bell in the tower of Santo Domingo tolled its funeral song. The whole city of Lima was in mourning. Yet in the hearts of those who thronged the church and convent, who stood looking at Martin de Porres for the last time, was one happy thought:

"We have known a saint!"

New York City
Feast of St. Thomas Aquinas
March 7, 1942

Also by the same author . . .

6 <u>MORE</u> GREAT CATHOLIC BOOKS FOR CHILDREN

. . . and for all young people ages 10 to 100!!

1200 SAINT THOMAS AQUINAS—The Story of "The Dumb Ox." 81 pp. PB. 16 Illus. Impr. The remarkable story of how St. Thomas, called in school "The Dumb Ox," became the greatest Catholic teacher ever.   6.00

1201 SAINT CATHERINE OF SIENA—The Story of the Girl Who Saw Saints in the Sky. 65 pp. PB. 13 Illus. The amazing life of the most famous Catherine in the history of the Church.   5.00

1202 SAINT HYACINTH OF POLAND—The Story of The Apostle of the North. 189 pp. PB. 16 Illus. Impr. Shows how the holy Catholic Faith came to Poland, Lithuania, Prussia, Scandinavia and Russia.   11.00

1203 SAINT MARTIN DE PORRES—The Story of The Little Doctor of Lima, Peru. 122 pp. PB. 16 Illus. Impr. The incredible life and miracles of this black boy who became a great saint.   7.00

1204 SAINT ROSE OF LIMA—The Story of The First Canonized Saint of the Americas. 132 pp. PB. 13 Illus. Impr. The remarkable life of the little Rose of South America.   8.00

1205 PAULINE JARICOT—Foundress of the Living Rosary and The Society for the Propagation of the Faith. 244 pp. PB. 21 Illus. Impr. The story of a rich young girl and her many spiritual adventures.   13.00

1206 ALL 6 BOOKS ABOVE (Reg. 50.00)   THE SET: 40.00

Prices subject to change.

U.S. & CAN. POST./HDLG.: $1-$10, add $2; $10.01-$20, add $3; $20.01-$30, add $4; $30.01-$50, add $5; $50.01-$75, add $6; $75.01-up, add $7.

**At your Bookdealer or direct from the Publisher.
Call Toll Free 1-800-437-5876**

MARY FABYAN WINDEATT

Mary Fabyan Windeatt could well be called the "storyteller of the saints," for such indeed she was. And she had a singular talent for bringing out doctrinal truths in her stories, so that without even realizing it, young readers would see the Catholic catechism come to life in the lives of the saints.

Mary Fabyan Windeatt wrote at least 21 books for children, plus the text of about 28 Catholic story coloring books. At one time there were over 175,000 copies of her books on the saints in circulation. She contributed a regular "Children's Page" to the monthly Dominican magazine, *The Torch*.

Miss Windeatt began her career of writing for the Catholic press around age 24. After graduating from San Diego State College in 1934, she had gone to New York looking for work in advertising. Not finding any, she sent a story to a Catholic magazine. It was accepted—and she continued to write. Eventually Miss Windeatt wrote for 33 magazines, contributing verse, articles, book reviews and short stories.

Having been born in 1910 in Regina, Saskatchewan, Canada, Mary Fabyan Windeatt received the Licentiate of Music degree from Mount Saint Vincent College in Halifax, Nova Scotia at age 17. With her family she moved to San Diego in that same year, 1927. In 1940 Miss Windeatt received an A.M. degree from Columbia University. Later, she lived with her mother near St. Meinrad's Abbey, St. Meinrad, Indiana. Mary Fabyan Windeatt died on November 20, 1979.

(Much of the above information is from Catholic Authors: Contemporary Biographical Sketches *1930-1947, ed. by Matthew Hoehn, O.S.B., B.L.S., St. Mary's Abbey, Newark, N.J., 1957.)*